Special Needs in the General Classroom:
Strategies that make it work

Susan Gingras Fitzell, M.Ed.

Cogent Catalyst Publications

Library of Congress Cataloging-in-Publication Data

Fitzell, Susan Gingras
     Special Needs In The General Classroom: Strategies That Make It Work 181 pp.
ISBN 1-932995-00-5

If you have questions or would like
Customized school in-service or ongoing consultation
Contact
Susan Gingras Fitzell
PO Box 6182
Manchester, NH 03108-6182
603-625-6087 or 210-473-2863

sfitzell@aimhieducational.com
www.aimhieducational.com

For supplemental handouts and information:
www.aimhieducational.com/inclusion.html

Other selected titles by Susan Gingras Fitzell, M.Ed.

- *Transforming Anger To Personal Power: An Anger Management Curriculum for Grades 6-12*
- *Please Help Me With My Homework: Strategies for Parents and Caregivers*
- *Free the Children: Conflict Education for Strong Peaceful Minds*
- *Umm... Studying? What's that? Learning Strategies for the Overwhelmed and Confused College and High School Student*

DEDICATION

To my students
at Londonderry High School
who have taught me so much over the years.

I'd also like to express my sincere appreciation to
Carol Woydziak
for her meticulous editing.
Hopefully, I got all the edits in correctly!

TABLE OF CONTENTS

OVERVIEW AND OBJECTIVES.. 1

GOOD FOR ALL, CRITICAL FOR DIVERSE LEARNERS.. 5

A MATTER OF PERSPECTIVE 5
THE SCHOOL HOUSE MODEL 6
DIFFERENTIATED INSTRUCTION 7
MULTIPLE INTELLIGENCES.. 8
BRAIN BASED LEARNING TECHNIQUES 10
    Questions and Answers about Brain Research 10
    12 Brain Based Learning Principles 11
    Brain Based Tips for the Classroom 13
PERSONALITY PREFERENCE AND LEARNING STYLE 14
    Characteristics of Type 14
    Something to Think About: Type & Learning Style 21

COLLABORATION & TEAMWORK 22

TOOLS FOR COLLABORATIVE RELATIONSHIPS 22
    Communication: What's Working? Card 22
    Tips for Successful Collaboration.. 23
    Pick-Me-Ups, Pick-U-Ups 23
    When In Conflict... 23
COLLABORATION MODELS 23
    Special Education Teacher as consultant.. 23
    The Co-teaching Model 24
PLANNING TIME... 25
PARAPROFESSIONALS.. 26
    A Paraprofessional's Point of View 27

CLASSROOM MANAGEMENT TECHNIQUES... 28

MANAGEMENT TOOLS, PROCESS & ENVIRONMENT 28
    Proactive Behavior Plans 28
    Basic Discipline Format... 29
    Music to Enhance the Learning Environment 30

CREATING CARING INCLUSIVE COMMUNITIES 31

PHYSICAL STRUCTURE AND ENVIRONMENTAL VARIABLES 31
CONFLICT EDUCATION AND BULLY PREVENTION 32
    The importance of Providing Structure and Consistency 32
    Establish a 'No Putdown Rule'-- a 'Safe Place' Environment................................. 33
    Emotions and Learning.. 34
STRATEGIES THAT FOSTER CARING INCLUSIVE COMMUNITIES....................... 34

Cooperative Learning..34
Peer Tutoring 35
Peer Leadership Training...36
Circle of Friends 37
   Circle Of Friends Basic Format: 37

STRATEGIES THAT PROMOTE SUCCESS **39**

USEFUL FORMS FOR PLANNING AND MAKING ADAPTATIONS 39
   Class List Adaptation Chart..39
   I.E.P. Based Planning Form 39
   Differentiated Planning – Lesson Planner 39
CLASSROOM & STUDENT ORGANIZERS...40
   Photocopies of Today's Notes 40
   Supplemental Reinforcement Materials..40
   Additional Copy of Assignments..40
   Homework Tip 40
   Assignment Board/Chart...41
TECHNOLOGY TOOLS..41
   Online Homework Bulletin Board...41
   Portable Text Editors 42
   Computerized Tools for Increasing Achievement 42
   Teacher Created Website to Supplement Instruction...................................43
   Text to Speech Software 43
ADAPTATIONS & ACCOMMODATIONS 44
   Adapt the Format of Handouts, Tests & Quizzes 44
      Make information and instructions Clear and Concrete 44
      Avoid Confusing Directions 45
      Clearly Define Expectations 47
      Use Points For Accountability And Motivation 48
      Provide Lines and Space 49
      Provide Checkboxes...51
      Make Special Accommodations—ENLARGE PRINT 53
      Adaptation Of Traditional World History Report: Provide Choice............55
      Math Tip For Spacial Difficulties 56
      Using Grids and Space to Teach Math 57
      Worksheet: Corporate Tax...58
      Half-sheet Theory 59
INTERVENTIONS AND ADAPTATIONS FOR STUDENTS WITH *AD(H)D*..................60
   Tips To Help Students Having Difficulty with Attention and Distractibility..................60
ADAPTATIONS FOR *AUDITORY PROCESSING DIFFICULTIES* 61
   A Solution for Students Who Rock Back and Fidget in Their Seats..............61
CONSIDERATIONS FOR STUDENTS IN THE *AUTISTIC SPECTRUM* 62

STRATEGIES THAT ENHANCE MEMORIZATION AND RECALL..............**63**

   Mind Mapping/Graphic Roadmaps/Visual Organizers 63
   Memory Models..65
   Mnemonic Devices 66

    Associations 66

    Rhyming... 66

    Chunking 67

    Acronyms 67

    Acrostics 67

  Strategy to Remember Sequences.. 68

  Color and Memory 69

    Draw It So You'll Know It 69

  Make It Meaningful 71

    Bring Emotion into the Lesson 71

    Attach It to Real Life: Instruction Guide with Students as Stars 72

  Who Am I? : Introduction or Review 73

  Zip Around 74

  Three Card Match: Review 75

  The Fitzpell Method of Studying Spelling Words 77

GRADING **78**

  GENERAL CONSIDERATIONS 78

    Options to Traditional Grading Systems.. 78

    What Constitutes a Lowered Grade? 79

    WHAT is Fair?.. 80

  ASSESSMENT ACCOMMODATIONS 81

    What is an Assessment Accommodation? 81

    Guiding Principles 81

    Types of Accommodations 82

  SPECIFIC TEST ADAPTATIONS 83

  GRADING OPTIONS 84

    Test Taking First Aid Kit 84

    An Alternative to the Traditional quiz 84

    Three Card Match: Peer Tutor or Peer Quiz 85

  CULTURE AND LANGUAGE BIAS AS BARRIERS TO LEARNING.................... 85

APPENDIX-- FAMOUS PEOPLE **88**

APPENDIX-- STRATEGIES THAT DIFFERENTIATE FOR ALL **90**

    Tip To Maintain Attention While Reviewing Instructions 90

  MULTIPLE INTELLIGENCES.. 91

  Differentiating for Multiple Intelligences 92

  PERSONALITY PREFERENCE/LEARNING STYLE 93

  Methods for *Teaching Introverts and Extroverts*.................................... 93

    TAPPS.. 93

    Nominal Group Method 93

    Think Pair Share 93

    Jig Saw 94

    Peer Practice Activity 95

    Teaching Each Other.. 96

    Marker Boards: So That All May Participate!... 96

Methods for *Teaching Sensing Type*s 97
   What Must Be Known (WMBK) Method 97
   KWHL METHOD 98
   The Application-Theory-Application A-T-A method 99
   Advanced Organizers as Defined by David Ausubel 99
   Provide a Syllabus 99
Methods for *Teaching Intuitives*: 101
   The Small Group Discover Method 101
   Overview Method 102
Methods for *Teaching Thinking Types* 102
Methods for *Teaching Feeling Types* 102
Methods for *Teaching Judging Types* 103
   Speed Writing 103
   Split Page 103
   Color Coding 103
   AOR Model 103
   Reverse Question 103
   Treating Objective Questions as Essay Question 103
Methods for *Teaching Perceptives* 104
   Use Audio Cassette Tapes for Feedback on Assignments 104
General Type Considerations for Teachers 104
TOOLS & TECHNIQUES THAT HELP STUDENTS FOCUS 105
Brain Gym® 105
   "Brain Buttons" 106
   "Hook-Ups" 106
   "Cross Crawl" 107
Mandalas as a Tool to Focus, Calm and Get Creative 107
   Color Your Own Mandala 108
READING COMPREHENSION STRATEGY 109
PARTICIPATION STRATEGIES 110
WRITING STRATEGIES 111
   Breaking Reports Down To The Writing Process 111
   Strategy for Getting "Un-stuck" While Writing: Clustering 113

APPENDIX --TEACHER TOOLS **121**

GOAL SETTING: A PROVEN MOTIVATIONAL STRATEGY 121
WIN-WIN DISCIPLINE PLAN 123
   Guidelines for Discussion: WIN-WIN Discipline Plan 124
   Example: Academic Support Rules and Procedures 125
CARING INCLUSIVE COMMUNITY TOOLS 126
   Classroom Management Cue Cards 126
   Problem Solving Mind Map 127
   Comebacks That Don't Escalate Conflict 128
TEACHER TOOLS: LETTERS AND FORMS 129
   Sample Letter to Students to Assist With Follow-Up 129
   Sample Letter to Teachers to Assist With Follow-Up 130
   "Quick Form" Letter to Teachers to Assist With Follow-Up 131

Class List Adaptations Chart 132
IEP Based Planning Form 133
Differentiated Planning: Lesson Planner 134
Homework Excuse Log 135

APPENDIX--STUDENT ORGANIZATIONAL TOOLS 137

NOTE TAKING STRATEGIES 137
Cut and Paste Notes Using Mind Maps and Charts 137
'Post It®' Note Method of Highlighting 139
Notebook Check 140
Landmark Notebook System 141
Three Column Note Paper 142
Method for Writing Better Sentences 143
Current Events 144
Book Report: 145
Grade Review Sheet 149

APPENDIX—LESSON PREP TOOLS 150

READABILITY FORMULAS 150
AUTOSUMMARIZE IN MSWORD 153
BLOOM'S TAXONOMY & QUESTIONING TECHNIQUE 154

APPENDIX –QUICK REFERENCE LISTS 156

SOCIAL STUDIES ADAPTATIONS 156
ENGLISH/LANGUAGE ARTS/FOREIGN LANGUAGE ADAPTATIONS 157
MATH ADAPTATIONS 158
PRACTICAL ARTS & P.E. ADAPTATIONS 159
SCIENCE AND HEALTH ADAPTATIONS 160
DIFFERENTIATED INSTRUCTION QUICK LIST 161
DIFFICULTY /ADAPTATION QUICK LIST 162
ADAPTATION QUICK LIST 163
SAMPLE I.E.P. PAGES 164
LEVELS OF SERVICES "BEST-PRACTICE" GUIDELINES 169

APPENDIX – RESOURCE LISTS 170

REFERENCE BOOKS AND RESOURCE ARTICLES 170
PRODUCT SUPPLIERS 172
CATALOGUES FOR RECORDED BOOK LOANS, RENTALS AND SALES 173
WORLD WIDE WEB RESOURCES 174
BRING SUSAN TO YOUR SCHOOL FOR CONSULTATION OR IN-SERVICE 178
ORDER SUSAN'S BOOKS! 179

NOTES: 180

1

Overview and Objectives

This book is designed to help you meet the challenges of teaching in an inclusive classroom. You will find techniques for collaboration between special education staff and classroom teachers, practical, proven ways to differentiate your teaching methods and materials to increase the effectiveness of your instruction and meet I.E.P. adaptations in the general classroom without reducing content. You will find teaching approaches, games, activities, and examples of adaptations to help your students become more successful in the inclusive classroom. These approaches and techniques work for ALL youth in the inclusive classroom and are critical for students with special needs.

A motto that works:

GOOD FOR ALL, CRITICAL FOR DIVERSE LEARNERS!

Visual Overview for the Conceptual Learner

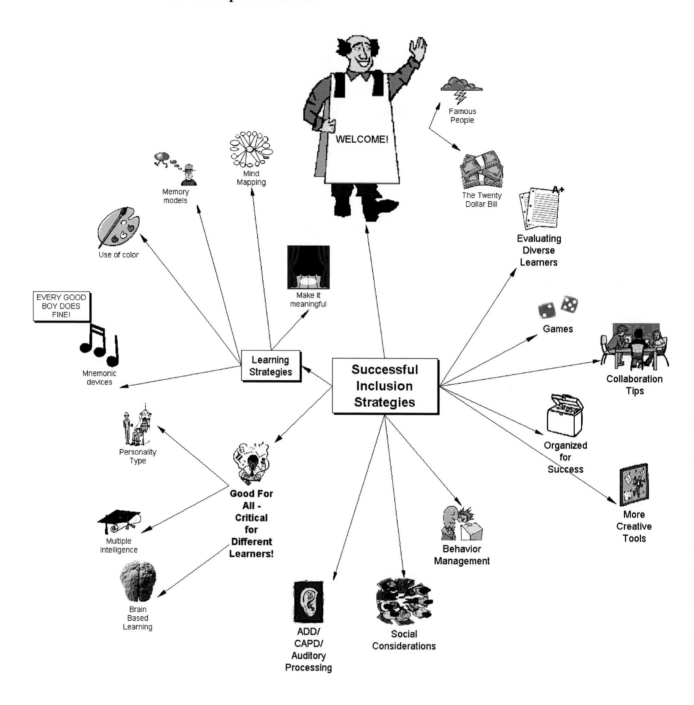

Famous People

The Twenty Dollar Bill

Evaluating Diverse Learners

Games

Collaboration Tips

Organized for Success

More Creative Tools

Behavior Management

Social Considerations

ADD/ CAPD/ Auditory Processing

Successful Inclusion Strategies

Good For All - Critical for Different Learners!

Brain Based Learning

Multiple Intelligence

Personality Type

Mnemonic devices

EVERY GOOD BOY DOES FINE!

Use of color

Memory models

Mind Mapping

Make it meaningful

Learning Strategies

WELCOME!

For the Linear Learner:

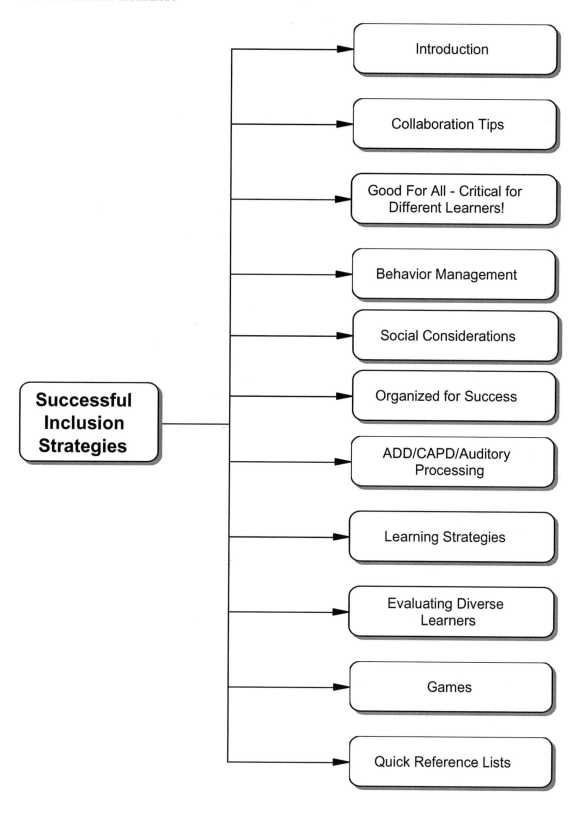

Before you begin reading this book, list what you already know about differentiating curriculum to meet the needs of all students in the classroom.

Then, list what you want to know.

What I know	What I want to know

When I attach new information to what I already know and am motivated by seeking answers to what I want to know—I learn.

Good for All, Critical for Diverse Learners

A Matter of Perspective

For over twenty-five years I have been working with students with learning differences. Sixteen of those years have been in public education. From my experience and knowledge based on extensive research on learning disabilities, brain-based learning, personality type, learning styles, and multiple intelligences, I propose the following as points of consideration and discussion:

- I firmly believe that many of the problems labeled as "learning disabilities" are actually learning differences. If we pay attention to students' learning styles, multiple intelligences, and brain based teaching techniques we will find ourselves more successful with <u>all</u> learners.

- Many students who do well in high school with minimal effort struggle in college because they lack the necessary study skills, organizational skills and memory strategies needed for the types of careers these bright young people are working towards: law, engineering, medicine, etc.

- When co-teaching with general classroom teachers, I found the most effective way to meet the needs of the learning disabled students in the classroom was to seek out ways that the general classroom teacher could implement adaptations quickly and easily. If I suggested an adaptation that worked for all the students in the classroom and did <u>not</u> reduce content, it would be more likely to happen. Consequently, <u>all</u> the students benefited.

- "Many educationally "different" children are bright and potentially talented. Few, if any, are "unteachable," but there is ample proof that plunging them abruptly into the chilly, analytic waters of mainstream instructional practices is a prescription for failure, frustration and a high dropout rate. The schools have three choices:

  1. Keep the traditional "standards" and continue to cram youth into them. Let prisons and the welfare system handle the overflow.

  2. Throw out the standards.

  3. Maintain the goals represented by the standards, but prepare students more effectively. Expand the schedule of expectation and the teaching methods to honor young people's latent abilities.

  The first two alternatives should be unthinkable. We are left with the third."

Excerpted From *Endangered Minds* by Jane M. Healy, Ph.D.

My approach to teaching diverse learners in the classroom is to meet their needs in the least obvious way possible so that they don't stick out as "different" and to create a learning environment where all students, including the gifted, benefit from the experience.

The School House Model

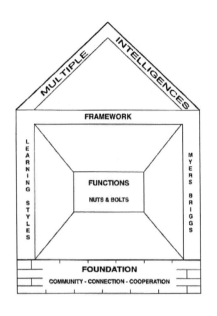

By Fritz Bell, Creative Classrooms, Raymond, NH

FOUNDATION:

In setting up an individual classroom or even an entire school itself, it is best to look at the School House Model. The base of the model is the foundation - **community, connection, and cooperation**. Many schools and individual classrooms forget this foundation and then wonder why the students can't work or learn together. It is important to have a strong foundation. We can look at Maslow's hierarchy of needs and see that four out of the five needs (physiological, safety, social, and self-esteem) are concerned with this area of foundation.

FRAMEWORK

The framework for the individual classroom or entire school should be based on an understanding of learning styles and multiple intelligences. If the teacher and students understand the differences in how they learn and make decisions based on that understanding, then they can progress to the self-actualization need that Maslow describes and learning can happen.

FUNCTIONS

The center of the School House Model is the functions or nuts and bolts. This is the actual curriculum and academic elements that should be taught. However, if the teacher or school only focuses on the functions and disregards both the foundation and framework, then the student will have a difficult time learning and retaining the knowledge presented.

When training teachers, if they are only presented with the functions and do not have a foundation and framework, they will not be able to create new ideas and lesson plans on their own but will only be able to try and replicate the functions that have been presented to them.

Differentiated Instruction

Differentiated instruction is an approach to planning in which lessons are taught to the entire class while meeting the individual needs of each child. This is accomplished by consistently planning lessons using strategies that meet the needs of all learners in the classroom. The content, process (instructional strategies), and product are the means by which the teacher meets the needs of all the students. The teacher determines the process according to the student's readiness level, interests, and learning profile.

EACH LESSON

▪ Has a definite goal for all students. ▪ Includes a variety of teacher techniques aimed at reaching students at all levels. ▪ Considers student-learning styles in presentation of lesson. ▪ Involves all students in the lesson using questioning aimed at different levels of thinking (Bloom's Taxonomy).	▪ Challenges students with respectful work based on their individual readiness level. ▪ Provides choice in the method students will use to demonstrate understanding. ▪ Accepts that different methods are of equal value. ▪ Evaluates students based on their individual differences.

STEPS:

1. *Identify Goals:*
- Content - What do all students need to understand? Separate content from process.
- Individual student objectives.

2. *Method of presentation:*
- Content is presented using methods that facilitate all students gaining varying degrees of knowledge based on their level of understanding.
- Cognizant of student learning style, multiple intelligences.
- Attending to level of cognitive domain - Bloom's Taxonomy (questioning techniques critical).
- Differentiated participation - based on student's skill level.
- Adaptations may be necessary to the environment, the materials, and the mode of presenting the information.

3. *Method of student practice:*
- Assignments based on student's needs.
- Consistent with learning style of student.
- Appropriate for level of cognitive ability - Bloom's Taxonomy.
- Differentiated participation - based on student's skill level.

4. *Method of evaluation:*
- Linked to identified goals.
- Considers learning styles of student.
- Considers level of cognitive ability - Bloom's Taxonomy.
- Differentiated participation - based on student's skill level.

Multiple Intelligences

Psychologist Howard Gardner identified the following distinct types of intelligence in his book, *Frames of Mind*. According to his theory, all people possess eight distinct sets of capabilities. Gardner emphasizes that these capabilities/intelligences work together, not in isolation. The intelligences, including his newest finding, the Naturalist, are:

Linguistic: Young people with this kind of intelligence use words effectively, either orally or in writing. They enjoy writing, reading, telling stories, or doing crossword puzzles.

Logical-Mathematical: Children have the capacity to use numbers effectively and to reason well. They are interested in patterns, categories, and relationships. They are drawn to arithmetic problems, strategy games, and experiments.

Bodily Kinesthetic: Children with this capability are experts in using their whole body to express ideas and feelings. They are good with their hands. These kids process knowledge through bodily sensations. They are often athletic, dancers, or good at crafts such as sewing or woodworking.

Spatial: These young people think in images and pictures. They may be fascinated with mazes or jigsaw puzzles, or spend free time drawing, building with construction sets, or inventing.

Musical: Musical students have the capacity to perceive, discriminate, transform, and express musical forms. They often spend time singing or drumming to themselves. They are usually quite aware of sounds others may miss. These kids are often discriminating listeners.

Interpersonal: These students have the ability to perceive and make distinctions in the moods, intentions, motivations, and feelings of other people. They are often leaders among their peers, who are good at communicating and responding to others' feelings.

Intrapersonal: These students are insightful and self-aware. They can adapt to their environment based on their understanding of themselves. These students may be shy. They are very aware of their own emotions, strengths, and limitations and have the capacity for self-discipline.

Naturalist: The core of the naturalist intelligence is the human ability to recognize plants, animals, and other parts of the natural environment, like clouds or rocks. These students have the ability to identify and classify patterns in nature. These students are sensitive to changes in the weather or are adept at distinguishing nuances between large quantities of similar objects.

Existentialist: Students who learn in the context of where humankind stands in the "big picture" of existence. They ask "Why are we here?" and "What is our role in the world?" This intelligence is seen in the discipline of philosophy.

> MI cannot be an educational end in itself. MI is, rather, a powerful tool that can help us to achieve educational ends more effectively. From my vantage point, MI is most useful for two educational ends:
>
> - It allows us to plan educational programs that will enable children to realize desired end states (for example, the musician, the scientist, the civic-minded person).
>
> - It helps us to reach more children who are trying to understand important theories and concepts in the disciplines.
>
> So long as materials are taught and assessed in only one way, we will reach only a certain kind of child. But everything can be taught in several ways. The more that we can match youngsters to congenial approaches of teaching, learning, and assessing, the more likely it is that those youngsters will achieve educational success.
>
> --- From an Interview with Howard Gardner by Ronnie Durie

References:
- Gardner, Howard. (1985). *Frames of Mind: The Theory of Multiple Intelligences.* (Paperback ed.). Basic Books.
- Gardner, Howard. (1987). *The Theory of Multiple Intelligences.* Annals of dyslexia, pp. 19-35.
- Gardner, Howard. (1990 Spring). *The Difficulties of School: Probable Causes, Possible Cures.* Daedalus, pp.85-114.

Brain Based Learning Techniques

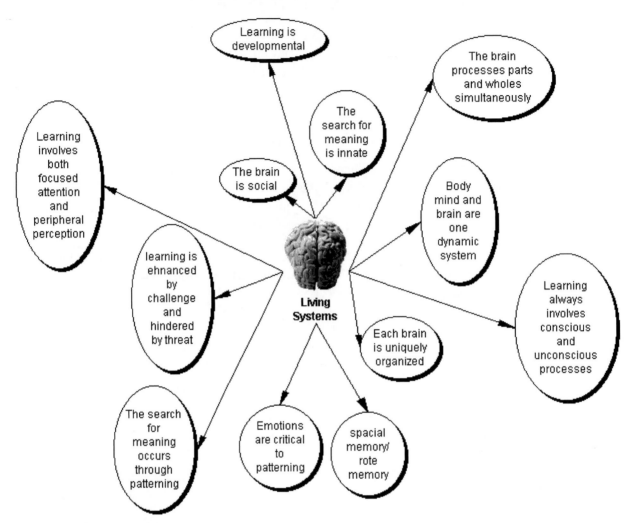

QUESTIONS AND ANSWERS ABOUT BRAIN RESEARCH

The brain reacts to shape, color, sound, texture, and light, yet teachers in the upper grades through high school still tend to teach through lecture-- verbal linguistic methods. Focusing on language-based teaching nourishes the left side of the brain but ignores the right side, which is dedicated to creative thinking.

Who Is Doing Brain Research?
Studies on the brain depend on research generated from the fields of molecular biology, psychoneuropharmacology, neurobiology, and neuroscience. The tools of exploration improve annually with advancements in computer technology and more precise methods of observing actual brain functioning as opposed to postmortem studies.

How Do Scientists Research the Brain?

Scientists use electrodes and amplifiers to map the brain's electrical activity. These studies are illuminating the sophisticated communication system established between brain cells. Neurobiologists study the communication between brain chemicals and the rest of the body's nervous system. Neuroanatomists use electronic microscopes to trace the neural pathways from deep within the brain all the way down to the big toes.

Does Brain Research Prescribe Proven Methods of Instructions?

Neuroscience lends credibility to many principles of good instruction, but this field does not purport to prescribe specific ways to teach or a new and improved curriculum. Much of the work on the brain is applied from laboratory studies using mice, kittens, primates, fruit flies, samples of fetal tissue, and others. Educators must use caution when choosing teaching methods: don't throw the baby out with the bathwater (in comes brain based out goes everything else, or visa versa). Yet, there is significant evidence to warrant encouraging those charged with rearing and educating young children to carefully tend to the brain's intrinsic need for meaningful experience, nurturance, and safety.

Adapted from "Decade of the Brain" by Jeri Levesque, Ed. D., Webster University School of Education, St. Louis, January 2000

12 BRAIN BASED LEARNING PRINCIPLES

Renate Nummela Caine and Geoffrey Caine identified basic patterns of how human beings learn. They call these the Twelve Principles of Brain Based Learning.[1] To summarize, there are at least twelve principles of brain-compatible learning that have emerged from brain research.

1. Uniqueness – every single brain is totally unique and becomes more unique as we age.

2. A threatening environment or stress can alter and impair learning and even kill brain cells.

3. Emotions are critical to learning – they drive our attention, health, learning, meaning, and memory.

4. Information is stored and retrieved through multiple memory and neural pathways that are continually being formed.

5. All learning is mind-body – movement, foods, attentional cycles, drugs, and chemicals all have powerful modulating effects on learning.

6. The brain is a complex and adaptive system – effective change involves the entire complex system.

7. Patterns and programs drive our understanding – intelligence is the ability to elicit and to construct useful patterns.

8. The brain is meaning-driven – meaning is more important to the brain than information.

9. Learning is often rich and non-conscious – we process both parts and wholes simultaneously and are affected a great deal by peripheral influences.

---

[1] http://www.cainelearning.com/principles.html

10. The brain develops better in concert with other brains – intelligence is valued in the context of the society in which we live.

11. The brain develops with various stages of readiness.

12. Enrichment – the brain can grow new connections at any age. Complex, challenging experiences with feedback are best. Cognitive skills develop better with music and motor skills.

How We Learn According to Brain Research

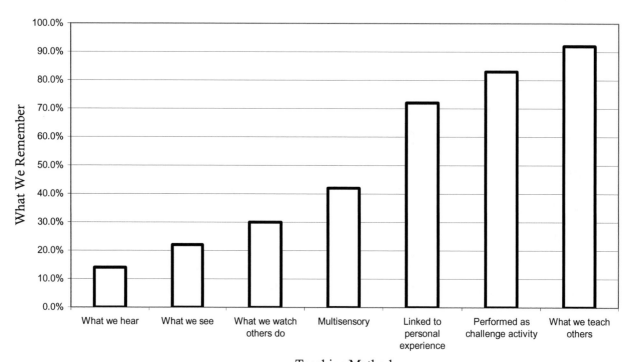

Sources:
Leonard. 1994.
Glasser. Control Theory in the Classroom. 1996
Dryden, Gorden & Vos, Dr. Jeannette. The Learning Revolution: A Life-Long Learning Program for the World's Finest Computer Your Amazing Brain. 1994.

BRAIN BASED TIPS FOR THE CLASSROOM

- Dim the lights if possible, or use blue, green, pink, or full spectrum lighting in the classroom.
- Play classical music -- Classical music connects with the brain, enabling students to learn better and to relax. Music should have less than 60 beats/minute.
- Give students choices.
- Use color.
  - Alternate color of bullets on overhead, whiteboard, and chalkboard.
  - Use color border for information that you want students to notice or remember.
  - Border printed spelling words to accentuate the "shape" of the word.

- Allow opportunity for expressing emotions and listening to others' feelings.
- Take more stretch breaks and when possible incorporate brain stimulating movement.
- Drink water -- The brain needs hydration. Students need at least 40 ounces of water a day.
- Print notes and study cards: avoid cursive for study.
- Relate learning to real world experiences: Make it meaningful.
- Reduce stress in the classroom – Stress hinders learning. Students perform best when they do not feel they are competing with each other for the highest grades.
- Use the "Power of Two" (work partners) for pulse learning.
- Use learner imposed deadlines.
- Use graphic organizers, group and classify, and teach through telling stories!

For resources on Brain-Based Learning and Strategies, see the Appendices.

Four Powerful Teaching Tips

Tip #1: Provide Meaningful Visual Cues
Tip #2: Provide Opportunity to Move!
Tip #3: Provide Opportunity to Share
Tip #4: Use Color to Present Instruction

Personality Preference and Learning Style

The MBTI reports a person's preferred way of 'being' in the world and his or her preferred process for making decisions.

CHARACTERISTICS OF TYPE

- There are polar opposites for each preference and each is useful and important.
- Your preferences for certain mental habits are a persistent part of your personality.
- There are no good or bad types.
- Psychological type is not an intelligence test.
- Everyone is an individual; type only helps us understand part of our personality (and learning style).
- The MBTI is an indicator. It indicates preference. It is not a test.

Following is a description of the four scales reported in the Myers-Briggs Type Indicator (MBTI), and several teaching approaches that will appeal to different MBTI profiles.

Sensing (S) versus Intuition (N)

Sensing types rely on their five senses. Sensing people are detail oriented, want facts, and trust them.

Intuitives rely on their imagination and what can be seen in "the mind's eye." Intuitive people seek out patterns and relationships among the facts they have gathered. They trust hunches and their intuition and look for the "big picture."

> **"Sensing types help intuitives keep their heads out of the clouds,
> while intuitives help sensing types keep their heads out of a rut."**

Judging (J) versus Perceptive (P)

Judging types prefer to make quick decisions. *Judging* people are decisive, planful (they make plans), and self-regimented. They focus on completing the task, only want to know the essentials, and take action quickly (perhaps too quickly). They plan their work and work their plan. Deadlines are sacred. Their motto is: just do it!

Perceptive types prefer to postpone action and seek more data. Perceptive people are curious, adaptable, and spontaneous. They start many tasks, want to know everything about each task, and often find it difficult to complete a task. Deadlines are meant to be stretched. Their motto is: on the other hand.

> **"Judging types can help perceiving types meet deadlines,
> while perceiving types can help keep judging types open to new information."**

Using your colored markers, draw picture or symbol to represent the Eight Personality Types/Learning Styles described on the previous pages *while you are reading.* *"Draw it so you'll know it!"*

SENSING	INTUITIVE
JUDGING	PERCEIVING

Thinking (T) versus Feeling (F)

Thinking types prefer to decide things impersonally based on analysis, logic, and principle. Thinking students value fairness. What could be fairer than focusing on the situation's logic, and placing great weight on objective criteria in making a decision?

Feeling types prefer to make decisions by focusing on human values. Feeling students value harmony. They focus on human values and needs as they make decisions or arrive at judgments. They tend to be good at persuasion and facilitating differences among group members.

> **"Thinking types need to remember that feelings are also facts that they need to consider, while feeling types need to remember that thinking types have feelings too!"**

Extraversion (E) versus Introversion (I)

This preference tells us how people "get their energy."

Introverts find energy in the inner world of ideas, concepts, and abstractions. They can be sociable but need quiet to recharge their batteries. Introverts want to understand the world. Introverts concentrate and reflect. Their motto is: Ready, Aim, Aim... For the introvert, there is no impression without reflection.

Extraverts find energy in things and people. They prefer interaction with others, and are action oriented. Extraverts are spontaneous thinkers who talk their thoughts aloud. Their motto is: Ready, Fire, Aim. For the extravert, there is no impression without expression.

> **"If you don't know what an extravert is thinking, you haven't been listening. But, if you don't know what an introvert is thinking, you haven't asked!"**

Using your colored markers, draw picture or symbol to represent the Eight Personality Types/Learning Styles described on the previous pages *while you are reading.* "Draw it so you'll know it!

THINKING	FEELING
EXTRAVERSION	INTROVERSION

TEACHING SENSING STUDENTS

Sensing students prefer organized, linear, and structured lessons. Sensing preferences tend to produce linear learners. They tend to *test worse* than their actual knowledge; tend to *apply better* than their actual knowledge.

When presenting lessons, include specifics, facts, and details. Show why it is realistic and makes sense. Include real life applications and examples of where this has worked before.

Three suggested methods for organizing a lecture
- What Must Be Known (WMBK) Method
- The Application-Theory-Application A-T-A method
- Advanced Organizers

TEACHING INTUITIVE STUDENTS

The small group discovery method will appeal to intuitive students and will teach sensing students how to uncover general principles. In using this method, sensing and intuitive students should be combined in learning groups. The intuitive student can help the sensing student to discover the theory; the sensing student can help identify and marshal the facts of the exercise.

Intuitive students must have the big picture, or an integrating framework, to understand a subject. The big picture shows how the subject matter is interrelated. Intuitive students can develop reasonably correct concept maps or compare and contrast tables. Fortunately, sensing students can be taught to do the same.

- Give Intuitives an overview of the day's lesson(s) at the beginning
- Put in context.
- Mention several possibilities.
- Talk about innovative happenings and current events.

TEACHING JUDGING STUDENTS

We have found that the following hints on note taking and test taking help judging students learn more effectively.

- Speedwriting
- Split Page
- Color Coding
- AOR Model
- Reverse Question
- Treating Objective Questions as Essay Question
- Remind Judging types to check their answers and take a second look when solving problems.

Judging students often reach too-quick closure when analyzing cases.

TEACHING PERCEPTIVE STUDENTS

Perceptive students often postpone doing an assignment until the very last minute. They are not lazy. Quite the contrary, they seek information to the very last minute (and sometimes beyond).

Break assignments down into chunks with parts due at specific dates that lead up to the final due date. These deadlines will help to keep the perceptive types on target. It also allows you to give ongoing feedback to the student adding to the final quality of the assignment.

- Break down assignments
- Help students set goals
- Use audio tapes to give frequent feedback
- Teach them to use organizers

TEACHING THINKING STUDENTS

Thinking students like clear course and topic objectives. Clear course or topic objectives avoid vague words or expressions such as "students will appreciate or be exposed to." Rather, objectives need to be precise and action-oriented. Precise objectives clearly define the type of learning that will happen: rote, meaningful and integrated, or critical thinking. In action-oriented objectives, the verbs describe what students must do, not what teachers will do. Bloom's taxonomy provides guidelines for writing clear and meaningful objectives.

- List all the pros and cons when possible, in the lesson.
- Structure the class material logically.
- Be succinct. Teachers who ramble lose thinking students.

TEACHING FEELING STUDENTS

Feeling students like working in groups, especially harmonious groups. They enjoy the small group exercises such as TAPPS and the Nominal Group Method. To promote harmonious groups, provide students with guidelines on how to work best in a group.

- Be friendly and collaborative.
- Show the impact of whatever you are teaching on people, especially why it is important to the individuals involved.
- Express appreciation for student contributions.

TEACHING EXTRAVERTED STUDENTS

Extraverted students learn by explaining to others. They do not know if they understand the subject until they try to explain it to themselves or others. Extraverted students often say that they thought they knew the material until they tried to explain it to a fellow student. Only then did they realize they did not understand the subject.

- To engage extraverts, convey energy and enthusiasm about the topic.

- Allow time for participation and discussion.

Extraverted students enjoy working in groups. Consider in-class or outside-of-class group exercises and projects. Some suggested activities:

- Thinking Aloud Paired Problem Solving (TAPPS) method
- Nominal Group Method.
- Think Pair Share
- Jig Saw

These methods support learning through explaining but provide quiet time for introverted students.

TEACHING INTROVERTED STUDENTS

Introverted students want to develop frameworks that integrate or connect the subject matter. To an introvert, disconnected chunks are not knowledge; rather, they are merely information. Knowledge means interconnecting material and seeing the "big picture."

To engage Introverts

- Provide written materials ahead – especially if you want discussion or decisions immediately.
- Pause when asking for response – 20 seconds is effective (but hard for Extroverts.)
- Be prepared to draw out some individuals with specific questions.
- Teach students how to *chunk,* or group and interconnect, knowledge. Introverted students will appreciate it although extraverted students may not. Nevertheless, cognitive psychologists tell us that through chunking, students master the material. It is also suggested that students learn to build a compare/contrast table, flowchart, or concept map when learning new material.

Additional Resources:

- The MBTI instrument is available from Consulting Psychological Press in Palo Alto, California.
- David Ausubel, **Educational Psychology: A Cognitive View**. Holt, Rinehart, and Winston, 1968.

See the Appendix for descriptions of teaching methods and techniques.

Information about Personality Preference and Learning style was adapted from *The Master Teacher*, by Harvey J. Brightman, Georgia State University, and *Implications of Personality Type for Teaching and Learning* by John W. Pelley, Ph.D., Texas Tech University Health Sciences Center, and the Myers-Briggs Type Indicator description pamphlets.

SOMETHING TO THINK ABOUT: TYPE & LEARNING STYLE

Eighty-five percent of students who drop out of school are Sensory Perceptive as measured by the Myers-Briggs Type Indicator and the Keirsey Temperament Sorter. Although they are 35-40% of the general population, only three percent of all teachers are of this personality type.

--Dr. Susan C. Francis

I may be your spouse, your parent, your offspring, your friend, or your colleague. If you will allow me any of my own wants, or emotions, or beliefs, or actions, then you open yourself, so that some day these ways of mine might not seem so wrong, and might finally appear to you as right -- for me. To put up with me is the first step to understanding me. Not that you embrace my ways as right for you, but that you are no longer irritated or disappointed with me for my seeming waywardness. And in understanding me you might come to prize my differences from you, and, far from seeking to change me, preserve and even nurture those differences.

--*Please Understand Me* II by David Keirsey

The most essential thing to know about the motivations of types is that thinking dominant types do their best work when pursuing logical order; feeling types do their best work when their heart is in it; sensing types do their best work when their practical skills are needed and valued; and intuitive types do their best work when pursuing an inspiration.

--*People Types and Tiger Stripes* Third Edition by Gordon Lawrence

I developed the SuccessTypes Survival Strategy as a realistic way of helping at-risk medical students improve their academic performance. If you are currently at-risk, you are dealing with several big problems at once. The root problem is probably not what you fear, that is, that you are not smart enough. Instead, the problem is probably in the way you learn, your learning style. Secondary problems are: 1) coping with the panic that sets in as the threat of failure becomes increasingly real, 2) coping with the challenge to your self identity as a successful student, and 3) coping with an increasing mountain of new material.

--John W. Pelley, Ph.D., author of "SuccessTypes for Medical Students"

3

Collaboration & Teamwork

Tools for Collaborative Relationships

In my professional experience the most effective way to meet the needs of students on an I.E.P. in the general classroom is to seek out ways that the general classroom teacher can implement adaptations quickly and easily. An adaptation that works for all students in the classroom and does not reduce content will more likely be embraced. Consequently, all students benefit.

COMMUNICATION: WHAT'S WORKING? CARD

Good communication with coworkers and students is critical to successful inclusion. Often, our fears, agendas, and even enthusiasm get in the way of doing the kind of listening we need to do to foster good communication. Without effective communication, we make many assumptions about the people with whom we interact. Those assumptions might be very inaccurate and create tremendous conflict. Try to keep an open mind. Express how you feel and listen to hear other points of views. Good communication is necessary for the success of an inclusive classroom.

```
It's Working!

Not Working ☹

Let's Try ....
```

This card is a simple way to give feedback to your co-workers or individual members of the teaching team. I found it to be useful for reinforcing the positives. It can be delivered in person, or placed in a teacher mailbox. Simple 3X5 index cards work well.

TIPS FOR SUCCESSFUL COLLABORATION	WHEN IN CONFLICT
■ Be flexible ■ Look for success not only in academic areas ■ Make time to plan – even if just 10 minutes! ■ Discuss problems only with each other ■ Avoid using red ink to write notes to your colleague PICK-ME-UPS, PICK-U-UPS ■ Compliment your colleague where all can see ■ Send a letter of appreciation and cc the principal ■ Remember special days with cards	■ Change negative self-talk to positive ■ Next time X happens… I'll do Y or Z ■ Plan viable solutions ■ Consider personality type ■ Seek suggestions from a supportive colleague or read Albert Ellis for suggestions to reframe ■ Visualize yourself in the interaction ***BEING SUCCESSSFUL***! ■ Affirm: "I CAN handle this situation"

Collaboration Models

SPECIAL EDUCATION TEACHER AS CONSULTANT

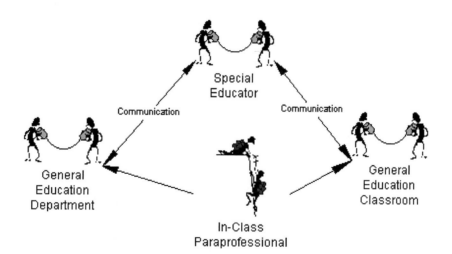

In this inclusion model the special education teacher acts as 'consultant' to the general classroom teachers. The special education 'consultant' works primarily outside the classroom with the general education teacher and may work directly in classrooms as needed. The general classroom teacher in this situation makes most if not all of the classroom adaptations, accommodations and modifications using the I.E.P. and the special educator as a guide and resource. If a paraprofessional is assigned to the general classroom, the special education teacher works closely with both the paraprofessional and the general classroom teacher.

THE CO-TEACHING MODEL[2]

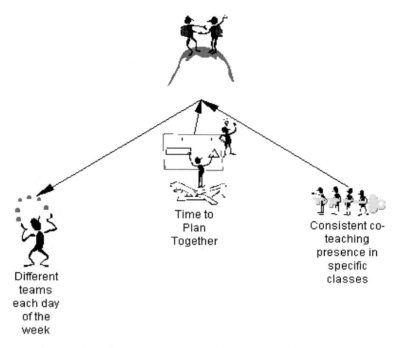

Time to
Plan
Together

Consistent co-
teaching
presence in
specific
classes

Different
teams
each day
of the
week

One Teacher, One Support Teacher ▪ Subject expert often lead teacher ▪ Support teacher often specialist	Support teacher's role defined by I.E.P.'s. The more time spent planning and collaborating, the more benefit to **all** in the classroom.
Station Teaching ▪ Divide content and students ▪ Each teach mini-class ▪ Then switch groups and repeat	It's important to not be hierarchical and to divide the student mix carefully so that both groups have a mix of students that works well together.
Parallel Teaching ▪ Divide the class ▪ Both teach same content to half the class ▪ Plan together for consistency	Here also, it's important to not be hierarchical and to divide the student mix carefully so that both groups have a mix of students that works well together.
Alternative Teaching ▪ One large group, one small ▪ Smaller group may need preteaching or reteaching, or challenge activities	This is a good approach to use a*s needed.* Having several small groups for different purposes would also eliminate some of the stigma of the L.D. student *always* being singled out.
Team Teaching ▪ Shared instruction and planning ▪ Coordinated activities ▪ Trust, commitment and personality compatibility a must	Many see this situation as the ideal, however, it primarily requires two teachers who are compatible in personality style, commitment, and teaching philosophy who also are given the time and support to plan together.

---

[2] Adapted from Friend, Marilyn & Cook, Lynne. *Interactions: Collaboration Skills for School Professionals. 4th ed.* : Allyn & Bacon, 1993

Planning Time

If you are working with a team, paraprofessionals or a co-teacher, you need time to plan together. If you don't have the time to discuss plans, review upcoming tests, consider recommended modifications and implementation of I.E.P. goals, it will be difficult, if not impossible, to have a successful inclusive classroom.

If your school provides you with planning time, stay focused on the task. Try to avoid social conversation because it will only leave you feeling as if you accomplished nothing afterwards. If possible, share information before hand through school mail so that the time you have can be used to the maximum benefit.

Speak up if you are being asked to give up planning time for other duties. You need that time and it is legitimate to require it.

If your school does not provide planning time, it will probably make your life easier in the long run if you can employ some of the following options:

- Use time before school, after school, or during common preps/specials to meet and plan. *Remember*: The goal is to make *YOUR* job easier and more successful long term. It is a waste of your energy to begrudge the time if you choose this option.
- Arrange for coverage with a substitute one day a week or month to free time to collaborate.
- Contact your local PTA and see if there are parent volunteers who may be willing to help cover classes so you can plan. High schools seriously under utilize volunteers.
- Oftentimes substitutes have free blocks of time when the teacher they are substituting for has prep periods. See if a substitute can cover your class during a free block of time.
- For information that must be communicated before the next school day, you might arrange to call each other after hours.
- Communicate through the mailbox or e-mail.
- If the regular classroom teacher can provide the special education staff person with copies of lesson plans, tests, projects ahead of time by simply photocopying and placing these items in the support teacher's mail box, it allows enough time for the specialist to assist with accommodations and make helpful recommendations. It also enables that person to go into the class prepared to help.
- Grade reports placed in the special education teacher's mailbox enable both the general classroom teacher and the special education teacher to catch failures before they become quarter grades.

Paraprofessionals

In-class assistance by paraprofessionals

Paraprofessionals in the classroom make the greatest contribution when they work directly with students. Too often, I have seen paraprofessionals used to run off papers, copy notes (solely), run errands, and hold up the back wall of the classroom. I found that when I treated my paraprofessionals as equals and involved them by requesting their suggestions and considering their input, the benefits to my class as a whole were significant.

Open communication, clarifying my expectations of the paraprofessional and working towards comfortable ground as a team was critical to our success in the Inclusive classroom. It was also extremely important for the students to see the paraprofessional as having authority in the classroom. I did not undermine my paraprofessional's position as an authority and I did not allow the paraprofessional to undermine my authority. If the students see this teacher-para team as divided, they will take full advantage and play one person off the other to the demise of the adult relationships and the success to the Inclusion class.

Often, paraprofessionals can provide the following services in the classroom:

- Copy notes
- Work in small groups
- Cue/refocus/redirect students
- Copy overheads
- Create worksheets using the *White-Out Method*
- Assist with the testing process
- Follow-up with the student outside the classroom
- Motivate and support students with homework
- Work with drop-in center, learning center, study lab to help students to focus and stay on track
- Ask questions in class
- Answer questions in class
- Share an opposite point of view
- Position control (This is what I called positioning oneself in the classroom as a behavior management strategy.)
- Assist with note taking
- Read orally (low level readers)
- Review for tests with small groups of students
- Guide student centered activities

Teamwork between the paraprofessional and the classroom teacher is an essential ingredient to a successful inclusion classroom. When a paraprofessional is assigned to a class, he or she should be seen as a part of the solution and not as an intrusion. Ideally, the paraprofessional and the classroom teacher have some common planning time to discuss upcoming assignments, progress of students and methods to help the students succeed. Without this time, it is difficult to establish a strong working relationship; however, the relationship can still be beneficial.

Paraprofessionals can be valuable resources in the classroom. They can work in class with students who are having difficulty understanding the information, provide notes for those students who are unable to take comprehensive notes during class time, and provide help with test and assignment modifications for students with learning disabilities.

Student follow-up is especially important to meet I.E.P. requirements and promote success. Often, the paraprofessional can follow-up in the resource room as well as in class. Paraprofessionals can support the classroom teacher by answering the questions of all students.

Paraprofessionals are an integral and important part of the classroom team. They are happy to contribute whatever they can to add to the success of all the students. If the teacher is accepting of the paraprofessional's presence, then the students will also accept it as normal and will consider him or her as the extra, valuable resource he or she is.

Ginger Davis
Londonderry High School

4

Classroom Management Techniques

Management Tools, Process & Environment

PROACTIVE BEHAVIOR PLANS

*Note: The text below was excerpted from *Free the Children: Conflict Education for Strong Peaceful Minds* and is geared towards ages K-12. The term "child" refers to older students and teens as well as younger children. This approach is very effective with adolescents.

Reality Therapy is a method of counseling developed by William Glasser, MD, which teaches people how to take control of their own lives, make more effective choices, and develop the strength to handle daily stresses and problems. At its foundation is the idea that regardless of what has happened to us or what choices we have made in the past, we can make different choices today and in the future to help us meet our basic needs. By making choices to change behavior, we can change our thinking and feelings.

Choice Theory is based on the fundamental belief that all humans choose behaviors in an attempt to fulfill five basic needs. According to Glasser, these needs are built into our genetic structure. Glasser identifies these basic needs as Love/Belonging, Freedom, Fun, Power, and Survival. Given this theory, human behavior is determined to be internally motivated. Therefore, the only person's behavior we can control is our own.

Although each of us possesses the same five basic human needs, each of us fulfills these needs differently. We develop an inner 'picture album' of how we see the world and what we want that world to be. Our behavior is an attempt to create the ideal world of our 'picture album'. A parent or teacher's goal is to get students to evaluate their present behavior and determine whether it is meeting their needs.

In one example, a teacher or parent might ask a child "Is your behavior getting you what you want?" If the child is talking constantly in class and as a consequence, loses his recess, the child who wants Love/Belonging is not getting what he wants through his behavior. On the contrary, he is losing that very thing at recess. If the child is not getting what he needs with his present behavior, he will make a specific plan for change and make a commitment to follow through.

The goal is for the child to determine that his current behavior is not getting him what he wants, and for *him* to choose other behaviors that will better meet his needs. The adult in the situation does *not* do the choosing for the child. The adult may offer suggestions to help the child come up with solutions, but, ultimately, the child must make the choice and commit to it. In this way, the child owns his behavior and the consequences of that behavior. The child cannot come back later and say to the adult, "You did this to me!" or "It's your fault." The child has ownership. Ownership is a critical step in effective discipline and moral growth.

I have found the behavior management approach based on this theory quite successful in the classroom. It utilizes an approach that promotes self-discipline, problem solving, and moral growth. A time-out procedure is used in the behavior management model. This time-out procedure may seem unworkable in school situations where a time-out room or area is not available. I have found that working with students before school, and/or after school, to work out solutions and develop "Both Win Discipline Plans" can lead to fruitful results. Be creative. Another argument against this method is that it is time consuming. It is...in the beginning. Be willing to put in the time in up front. It will pay off in the end.

The most effective way to learn the behavior management approach based on Reality Therapy and Choice Theory is to take a weeklong intensive workshop. If intensive training is not available to you, the books listed under 'recommended reading' can help you get started.

BASIC DISCIPLINE FORMAT

- *First Offense:* Ask the student, "What are you doing? Is it against the rules? Can you follow the rules?" If the answers are acceptable, student and teacher resume their roles in the class.
- *Second Offense:* Same procedure.
- *Third Offense:* Ask the same questions, except end with the consequence: "You will need to make a [discipline] plan." Assign time to work out a plan with you. (Detention with teacher after school, before school or during a study/lunch period. Detention lasts as long as it takes to make the plan whether 5 minutes or repeated detentions over X amount of days.
- *OPTIONAL:* Sometimes students need to be removed from the room. Arrange with administration to have a time out area for students to "chill." It is often best to not have the administration interfere, but rather to support your efforts to work out the issue with the student yourself through the behavior planning process.

***Do not get pulled into bantering with the student. Do the steps above and walk away. Stick to the script.

For forms and instructions, see Appendix: Teacher Tools.

MUSIC TO ENHANCE THE LEARNING ENVIRONMENT

Mozart for Modulation Music to Enhance Attention and Learning, Selections by Sheila Frick, OTR-- (Audio CD)—

- Helps with attention issues and sensory processing difficulties
- Supports organized body movement
- Improves attention and spatial concepts
- Assists active engagement of the learner

Baroque for Modulation Selections to Enhance Attention and Learning
by Sheila Frick, OTR, Alexis Richter, and John Goodell. Audio CD.

- "Increases both alpha and beta brain waves which are associated with a quiet, alert state that is receptive for learning."
- Helps to provide structure for organized thinking, e.g. writing reports or papers, activities that involve planning.

How to Use Music in Your Classroom

1. Playing music can be a distraction especially when students are reading. Here are some guidelines:

2. Select a CD to fit the project your students are engaged in doing:

   - Learning, Concentration, and Thinking at 50-60 b.p.m. for study, testing, workgroups, and computer time.
   - De-Stress, Relax at 30-60 b.p.m. for settling the class after high energy activities or disruptions, or rest times
   - Inspiration, at 60-90 b.p.m. for creative work
   - Motivation at 120-140 b.p.m. and Productivity at 70-130 b.p.m. for task completion and kinesthetic activities.

3. Keep the volume low. You should not have to 'talk above' the music. The music should be in the background creating a filter for unwanted noise in the classroom throughout the day. This creates the body relaxed, mind alert state.

4. For a break after 45 minutes or more of studying, you may increase the volume a bit so that students may listen for a few minutes to the music. This technique is recommended in the book "Learn with the Classics" by Anderson, Marsh and Harvey. It is meant to relax students and let their minds reflect on what they have learned.

Adapted from Advanced Brain Technologies, LLC (ABT),
<http://www.advancedbrain.com/index.html>-- products available at this site.

5

Creating Caring Inclusive Communities

Each teacher has his or her own preference for class structure, consistency, and management. While it is important to understand that teachers must be free to be "themselves" and have their own styles of running their classroom, some teaching styles seem to lend themselves well to inclusive populations where others are more challenging for both students and teachers.

Consider:
- Consistency without rigidity
- Firm discipline without power struggles
- Reasonable flexibility without lax standards
- The goal of the lesson rather than the specifics of the process
- Learning as the goal, rather than focusing on "that" test grade (Retake a test?)

Physical Structure and environmental variables

- Change student seating (closer to center of instruction, closer to teacher, away from friends, away from distracters). Consider: a student chooses to change his/her seating as part of a win-win behavior plan. The student owns the behavior and the solution.
- Require distracting items/objects be put away and out of sight.
- Increase distance between desks and provide more space if possible.
- Try using music for transitions and for calming/relaxing students.
- Scan room frequently and stay alert to what students are engaged in at all times.
- Consider student's individual needs: vision issues, hearing issues, focus, and comfort levels.
- Avoid seating learning-disabled students together in the room as permanent seating. It singles them out for stigmatization (the stupid group) and creates a situation where they may feed off each other behaviorally.
- Consider having "fidget toys" available for kids that need to have something in their hands.

Conflict Education and Bully Prevention[1]

In my book, *Free The Children: Conflict Education for Strong, Peaceful Minds*, when I refer to conflict, I am referring to interpersonal conflict between two or more people. I describe what I teach as conflict education rather than as conflict resolution. I believe it is necessary to educate before there is a conflict. Much of the material available for teaching conflict resolution skills is simply what it says it is: activities that teach skills to deal with issues after there is already a conflict. Much of it is geared toward wide age ranges encouraging a pick and choose approach that does not lend itself to a comprehensive, developmentally appropriate process. I say process rather than program because teaching character and conflict education is not something that can be done in a set of isolated lessons in a curriculum program.

Through my research and experience, I have determined that five areas need to be addressed on a *continuous* basis to achieve long term results from a character & conflict education process. These five components are:
- Modeling: role modeling for youth
- Relationship: the connections with or between people - how we relate
- Conditioning: the effects of the environment on our youth
- Empowerment
- Skills: relationship, conflict resolution, and mediation

These five components are critical to an effective character and conflict education curriculum. They apply to all developmental levels. Without all five aspects in the curriculum on a consistent basis, long-term results cannot be achieved. These five components are discussed in *Free the Children: Conflict Education for Strong, Peaceful Minds,* New Society Publishers, 1997.

THE IMPORTANCE OF PROVIDING STRUCTURE AND CONSISTENCY

> **According to a Justice Department study, parental supervision, attachment to family, and consistency of discipline were the most important barriers to delinquency and drug abuse.**
> **—Stuart Greenbaum, "Drugs, Delinquency, and Other Data" 1993**

If we listened to what students say when they are disciplined, we would think that discipline is the last thing they want. We fear we might lose them if we discipline them too much. Or worse, they might turn on us. In one survey of children aged 10 to 17, however, 39 percent said they 'sometimes' wished their parents were stricter or kept a closer watch over them and their lives.(National Commission on Children, p. 15)[2]

---

[1] Excerpted from *Free The Children: Conflict Education for Strong, Peaceful Minds* by Susan Fitzell

[2] National Commission on Children. (1991). *Speaking of Kids: A National Survey of Children and Parents.* Washington, DC: Author.

Adolescents, especially between the ages of 13 through 16, need adults to set reasonable rules and limits and to stand firm regarding them. Teens will push back, kicking and screaming against the boundaries. If parents yield to them, they will eventually believe that their parents do not care (Staley 174)[3]. Teenagers admire strength, not weakness. They do not need a parental friend. They need a parent they will respect. I never worry that my students may not like me. What matters to me is that they respect me and believe me to be fair.

ESTABLISH A 'NO PUTDOWN RULE'-- A 'SAFE PLACE' ENVIRONMENT

Class rule: No putdowns, no exceptions not by students or by the teacher.

Considerations and logic behind the rule:
Sarcasm and put-downs have become an acceptable form of entertainment and humor in our society. Because of this cultural acceptance, people, young and old, rationalize that it is Okay to denigrate another person in the name of 'teasing", good-fun, and humor. Unfortunately, this belief system causes problems:

- There are people, students included, who cannot read the difference between sarcastic humor and intentional meanness. Many learning disabled students are in this group.
- Students learn best in a safe, non-threatening environment. How does the teacher draw the line between what is humor and what is bullying or mean?
- I used to tell my students, "Even if someone laughs at your teasing, how do you really know what they are feeling? Would most students, especially male students 'show' their hurt?" I talked to a young woman with an eating disorder who shared with me "one line"-- What someone said to her in the seventh grade sent her into the spiral of an eating disorder. She could pinpoint the putdown to that moment in time. Also, remember the student shooter in San Diego? He laughed off the putdowns he had to endure. Then he showed up at school with a gun.
- I ask, "How do we know that our words meant in fun are taken as they are meant?" Is it worth the risk?
- What if we encouraged our students to share when words came across as putdowns even when the person using the putdown is the teacher? What kind of environment would that create in our classrooms?
- Many adults who use sarcastic humor become very defensive when this rule is suggested. Why do you think that is? We need to ask ourselves, "What kind of room do I want to run? What kind of community do I want to create in my classroom? How do I achieve that?"
- People who use sarcasm as humor are not bad people. Rather, they are conditioned by their upbringing or our media culture to enjoy it, accept it, and use it. Awareness is the first step to change.

---

[3] Staley, Betty K. (1988). *Between Form and Freedom: A Practical Guide to the Teenage Years.* United Kingdom: Hawthorn Press.

EMOTIONS AND LEARNING

It is important for students to have time to deal with their emotions. Teenagers are often ruled by their emotions. Emotions override their good judgment, dominate their peer relationships, and physically exhaust them. If they find a new love, their world is an emotional high. If they break-up with a boyfriend or girlfriend, their distress can be all consuming. Arguments can become volatile. Protests are passionate. The fight for independence is powered by intense emotion. When teens are in a state of extreme emotion, it is difficult for them to focus on academics or household responsibilities. Often, they simply cannot function beyond talking endlessly with friends about their feelings or withdrawing to their room to sleep or listen to music.

A little patience and care can go a long way when teens are overpowered by the turmoil of their emotions. In the classroom, try to foster an environment where teens feel comfortable enough to ask for what they need, whether that means seeing a guidance counselor, the nurse, or a trip to the lavatory to pull themselves together.

It's easy for us to trivialize some of the problems about which teenagers get upset. To teenagers, however, their problems are all consuming. Their emotions are intense. They don't have the maturity to keep these things in perspective. They need us to be understanding, to give them space to deal with these emotions, but also to set boundaries and limits so that we are not victims of their outbursts and they are protected from clouded judgment.

Strategies that Foster Caring Inclusive Communities

COOPERATIVE LEARNING

WHAT IS IT? Cooperative learning is a successful teaching strategy in which small teams, each with students of different levels of ability, use a variety of learning activities to improve their understanding of a subject. Each member of a team is responsible not only for learning what is taught but also for helping teammates learn, thus creating an atmosphere of achievement.

WHY USE IT? Documented results include improved academic achievement, improved behavior and attendance, increased self-confidence and motivation, and increased liking of school and classmates. Cooperative learning is also relatively easy to implement and is inexpensive.

HOW DOES IT WORK? Here are some typical strategies that can be used with any subject, in almost any grade, and without a special curriculum:

GROUP INVESTIGATIONS are structured to emphasize higher-order thinking skills such as analysis and evaluation. Students work to produce a group project, which they may have a hand in selecting.

STAD (Student Teams-Achievement Divisions) is used in grades 2-12. Students with varying academic abilities are assigned to 4- or 5-member teams in order to study what the teacher has initially taught and to help each reach his or her highest level of achievement. Students are then tested individually. Teams earn certificates or other recognition based on the degree to which all team members have progressed over their past records.

JIGSAW II is used with narrative material in grades 3-12. Each team member is responsible for learning a specific part of a topic. After meeting with members of other groups, who are "expert" in the same part, the "experts" return to their own groups and present their findings. Team members then are quizzed on all topics. (Balkcom)[4]

A resource for Cooperative Learning and Inclusion:

Cooperative Learning and Strategies for Inclusion: Celebrating Diversity in the Classroom by JoAnne W. Putnam, editor, 1993 ISBN 1-55766-346-7

This 188-page book is intended to help educators meet the needs of children with varying cognitive abilities, developmental and learning disabilities, sensory impairments, and different cultural, linguistic, and socioeconomic backgrounds. It is based on the premise that children of differing abilities and backgrounds will benefit both academically and socially from cooperative learning. Order from Paul H. Brookes Publishing Company at www.brookespublishing.com.

> **"Benefits of cooperative learning that have been shown in research include improved academic achievement, increased self-confidence and motivation, and increased liking of school and classmates. In addition, cooperative learning strategies have been shown to be relatively easy to implement and to have such added benefits as increased critical thinking skills and teamwork among students, more positive relations among different ethnic groups, and improved behavior and attendance."**
> **http://www.gse.uci.edu/ed173/resources/lectures/unit4_lectures.html**

PEER TUTORING

One of the most successful approaches that I have used in the Inclusion classroom to reinforce material is peer tutoring. Ten to fifteen minutes a few times a week can make a significant difference in student test results.

Students work with each other on a one-to-one basis to reinforce vocabulary, content area facts, or application of material.

Some students initially need instruction on how to peer tutor; however, many students naturally know how to teach their peers. Students generally relate well to their peers and the social aspects of peer tutoring interaction allows them to feel less drudgery with the study process. In addition,

---

[4] Balkcom, Stephen. "Cooperative Learning." CONSUMER GUIDE OR 92-3054 ED/OERI 92-38. 20 Jun 2000 <http://www.ed.gov/pubs/OR/ConsumerGuides/cooplear.html>.

students benefit from the cheerleading, pushing, feedback, and clarification provided by their peers.

> Michael Webb in "Peer Helping Relationships in Urban Schools" (ERIC, 1987)[5] writes, "As a result of their efforts to help others, tutors reinforce their own knowledge and skills, which in turn builds their self-confidence and self-esteem. Peer tutors also develop a sense of responsibility as a result of helping students to learn. Finally, explaining the subject matter to others often helps tutors better understand it themselves.
>
> Both tutors and students being tutored have also reported improved attitudes toward school as a result of their participation.
>
> The use of peer tutors in the classroom can make teachers more flexible and enable them to better target their efforts toward individual students. They can introduce learning activities that could not be accommodated within their regular teaching load. Peer tutors, by assuming responsibility for the reinforcement of what has been covered in class by the teacher, or for remedial instruction, can free teachers for new roles as coordinators and facilitators instead of their functioning solely as dispensers of knowledge.
>
> Numerous studies have demonstrated the effectiveness of the peer tutoring relationship. Students in effective programs consistently reach higher levels of academic achievement than students in conventional learning, or mastery learning situations."

In addition to gaining mastery over academic material, peer tutoring offers students the opportunity to participate amongst their peers in a meaningful role. I have seen students who typically exhibit challenging behavior model caring, focus, attention to detail, and determination to succeed when in a peer tutoring situation. Peer tutoring, youth helping youth, builds self-esteem. It's also an exercise in contributing to society in a positive way, which is a wonderful life lesson.

For more activities conducive to cooperative learning and peer tutoring see Personality Preference Methods and other learning methods that involve pairs and or groups in the Appendix: Strategies that Differentiate

---

PEER LEADERSHIP TRAINING

- Establish a "for credit" course
- Begin with in-service training for all peer leaders
- Assign each peer leader to a "buddy"
- Peer leadership includes activities such as:
  - Invitation to lunch
  - After school activities

---

[5] ERIC Identifier: ED289949, Webb, Michael, 1987-12-00, ERIC Clearinghouse on Urban Education New York NY.

- Join buddy at a game or assembly
- Provide a network outside of school

CIRCLE OF FRIENDS

One method that has been very successful to integrate students into the general classroom is a process called circle of friends. Circle of friends involves including a range of peers from the classroom along with the student who needs assistance working together to help that student have friendships, learn social skills, and monitor his or her behavior. Teachers obtain permission from the parents to form a circle of friends. In the classroom, the peers help each other.

For instance, when they see the circle student doing something socially inappropriate or maybe beginning to act up, the peers cue their friend. These students often don't realize that they are on the verge of getting themselves in trouble. How powerful and effective it can be when peers can give a non-verbal cue…you are losing control.

- Involves a range of peers
- Student with special needs included
- Provides friendship
- Students learn social skills
- Friends provide assistance to each other.
- Encourages fellowship

CIRCLE OF FRIENDS BASIC FORMAT:

1. Draw four circles (see diagram).
2. In the innermost circle, list people that you love and are closest to.
3. In the second circle list people who are closest to you and whom you really like.
4. In the third circle list groups of people you enjoy doing things with but less often than those in circle two.
5. In the fourth circle list people who get paid to be in your life.
6. Ask students to share their circles.
7. Show an example of a circle for student without friends.
8. Discuss the circle. What do you think about the circle? How would you feel if your circle looked like this?
9. Ask for suggestions on ways the group could help the student without friends start to fill in his circles with friends.
- Arrange for ongoing meetings of circle of friends and assemble the group periodically to celebrate successes, and problem solve as necessary.

For more information go to: www.inclusive-solutions.com/frameset.htm
There you will find essential information and tracking forms.

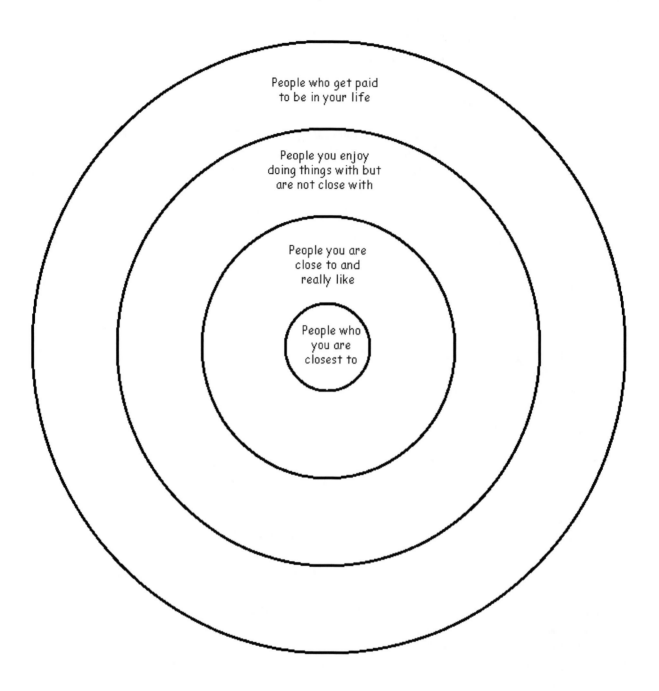

People who get paid
to be in your life

People you enjoy
doing things with but
are not close with

People you are
close to and
really like

People who
you are
closest to

Successful Inclusion Strategies

6

Strategies that Promote Success

Useful Forms for Planning and Making Adaptations

The following forms, available in the Appendix – Teacher Tools, assist teachers in keeping track of student I.E.P. requirements.

CLASS LIST ADAPTATION CHART

The "one sheet at a glance" adaptation list is a quick way to keep track of I.E.P. modifications and student considerations. It does *not* replace reading the I.E.P.

- Place the names of the students who have I.E.P.'s across the top of the chart.
- Check off the adaptations in the column under the students' names.
- Code special considerations as necessary.
- Reference this list before testing, assigning projects and as a daily reminder.
- It works well when placed in the plan book.
- If you put it in your plan book or grade book, be certain to not leave it where students might get to it.

I.E.P. BASED PLANNING FORM

The single student form helps plan for students with significant special needs and considerations.

DIFFERENTIATED PLANNING – LESSON PLANNER

The planning mind map helps teachers remember all aspects of planning for a differentiated classroom. Use it while you are planning to visually "cue" you into remembering what methods you might use to meet the needs of all learners in your classroom.

Classroom & Student Organizers

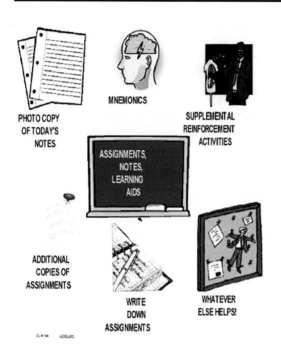

PHOTO COPY OF TODAY'S NOTES

MNEMONICS

SUPPLEMENTAL REINFORCEMENT ACTIVITIES

ASSIGNMENTS, NOTES, LEARNING AIDS

ADDITIONAL COPIES OF ASSIGNMENTS

WRITE DOWN ASSIGNMENTS

WHATEVER ELSE HELPS!

PHOTOCOPIES OF TODAY'S NOTES

Place a copy of the daily notes in a folder on the bulletin board or in a crate with file folders for each unit. It is a tremendous help to students who were absent, who are slow taking notes, who cannot listen to lecture and copy at the same time, or who are having an exceptionally bad day and consequently miss the notes.

I have students "copy" the photocopy unless their I.E.P. says they should not be expected to copy notes.

SUPPLEMENTAL REINFORCEMENT MATERIALS

ADDITIONAL COPY OF ASSIGNMENTS

Same idea as above. Place extra copies of assignments in a bulletin board pocket or a crate.

Add to the folders and crates, books on topic at lower reading levels, graphic organizers, visuals, study guides, audio tapes, video if available, anything supplemental that can help meet the learning styles and multiple intelligences of your students.

HOMEWORK TIP

Designate a consistent "spot" in the classroom for turning in homework and assignments. This simple accommodation can make a world of difference for students in the Autistic Spectrum and students who "forget" to turn in completed assignments.

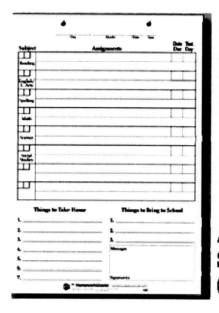

Available Through Success By Design (800) 327-0057

ASSIGNMENT BOARD/CHART

- Printed
- Listed with due dates
- Checkpoints
- Calendar format
       OR
- List format

A large write-on/wipe-off wall calendar works very well. Students can "see" time on a calendar and are less likely to misjudge how much time is left before an assignment is due. Color-code the calendar to match "assignment filled" manila folders in an organizational crate.

Technology Tools

ONLINE HOMEWORK BULLETIN BOARD

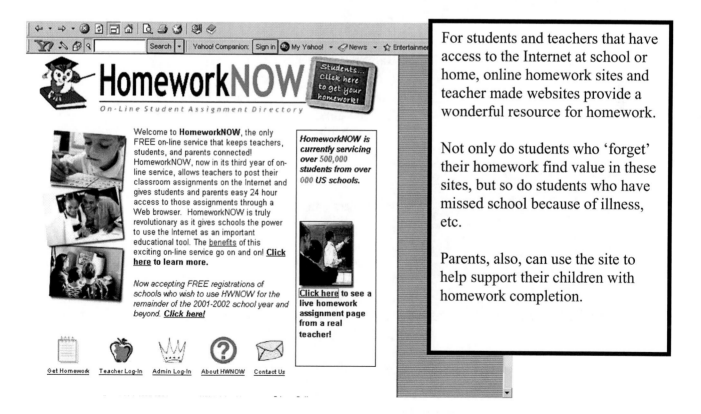

For students and teachers that have access to the Internet at school or home, online homework sites and teacher made websites provide a wonderful resource for homework.

Not only do students who 'forget' their homework find value in these sites, but so do students who have missed school because of illness, etc.

Parents, also, can use the site to help support their children with homework completion.

PORTABLE TEXT EDITORS

 There are a few portable text editors on the market currently. Compare capability, cost, and adaptability to your situation. One example is the AlphaSmart 3000, a simple, portable, and affordable computer companion. It is compatible with any computer, Macintosh or PC, and with most printers. It enables users to type, edit, and electronically store text (for example, reports, essays, email messages or notes), and to practice keyboarding, without having to be at a computer. The text can then be transferred to any computer for formatting, or directly to a printer. Its portability allows students to use it anywhere and anytime (for example, in the classroom, at home or on field trips). The AlphaSmart has an optional 100% error-free IR (infrared) interface that allows wireless transfer between the AlphaSmart and a computer or printer.

COMPUTERIZED TOOLS FOR INCREASING ACHIEVEMENT

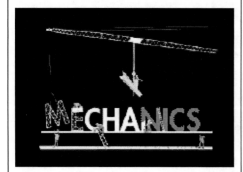

BRAINCHILD'S PLS1000 offers the core benefits of computer software on an inexpensive, portable device. Its hallmark feature is the "Explain" function that gives immediate feedback for every answer selection. The PLS 1000 is used extensively in extended learning programs with 6 strategies for giving students extra opportunities to learn. This works especially well when students have not succeeded in certain subjects with conventional instructional methods.

The PLS-1000 is used to:

Raise test scores
Provide equity and access
Create a school-to-home connection
Enrich with 6 extended learning strategies
Establish after school programs
Establish tutor programs

BRAINCHILD's Mechanics Series is a tool that allows students to catch up without embarrassment.

Students with special needs, on a 504 plan, or at risk and behind grade level on state testing and standards can use the Mechanics Series to improve quickly and individually while classroom teachers focus on varying academic groups. Students can practice on the bus, at home, and virtually ANYWHERE with this exciting tool!

www.aimhieducational.com/brainchild.html

TEACHER CREATED WEBSITE TO SUPPLEMENT INSTRUCTION

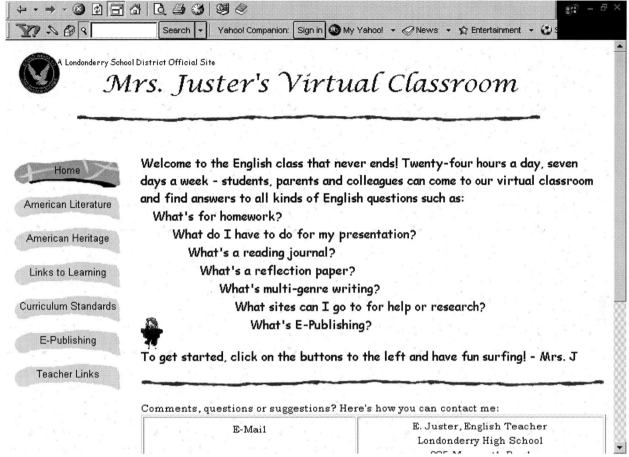

http://www.mrsjustersvirtualclassroom.com/

TEXT TO SPEECH SOFTWARE

There are several sources of software available with products, which allow you to scan or download text and convert the text to speech. Students who have difficulty reading can benefit greatly from this software.

The Kurzweil 3000, a PC-based reading system developed specifically for ease of use by students and teachers, is an ideal compensatory aid for individuals with reading difficulties. This application allows the user to view a scanned page on the computer screen while listening to the text being read aloud.
http://www.kurzweiledu.com/

ReadPlease®!
Developer of award-winning text-to-speech software for Windows® based operating systems.
http://www.readplease.com/

See the Appendix, *Resource Lists*, for MANY more technology solutions!

Adaptations & Accommodations

ADAPT THE FORMAT OF HANDOUTS, TESTS & QUIZZES

- Add a chart or present information in chart format.
- Add pictures or visual cues.
- Provide information in small chunks-- Keep facts on handouts and overheads to 5–7 with graphics.
- Provide Models--Have samples of previously made projects.
- Provide 3-D models of concepts being taught.
- De-clutter.
- It is better to have white space on the page than too much material. What you save in paper, you lose in learning.
- Simplify wording.
- Add Structure.
- Present information in sequential order.
- Use crosswords for review.
- Reword.
- Make the assignment hands-on.
- Provide an outline.
- Highlight Key points.
- Transfer word lists written on paper to index cards.
- Lower the reading level.

MAKE INFORMATION AND INSTRUCTIONS CLEAR AND CONCRETE

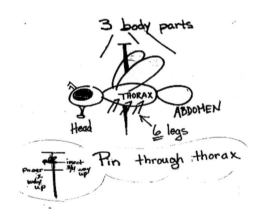

While pinning insects for an insect collection, some students needed to *see* the insect pinned as well as *hear* how to pin it.

This image has the water colored in so the land mass is spatially separate and different from the water

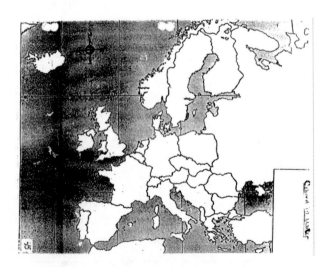

AVOID CONFUSING DIRECTIONS

Look for confusing directions in handouts, tests, and especially project descriptions. Even if unclear aspects are discussed in class, some students will miss the clarification. Provide the opportunity for success by insuring that the written instructions are very clear.

Often what is clear to us because *we* know what *we* are talking about is not necessarily clear to someone else. Imagine how confusing this is for the special needs student!

- Look for confusing directions in ready-made handouts.
- On worksheets, put each specific instruction with the activity being instructed.
- Do not put all the instructions for one worksheet at the top of the page with two or three activities below it when each activity requires a different instruction.
- Use simple terminology in the instructions. Words with double meanings cause confusion. Some students will do poorly on a test or activity because they did not understand the language in the instructions.
- Break instructions down into bullets. Paragraph form invites the student to miss instructions.
- Provide examples whenever possible.
- When assigning projects, provide models of the completed project for kids to use as guide. How often do we, as adults, need to **see** examples of resumes, letters, finished décor, constructed furniture, **before** we can do it ourselves? Yet, we routinely require students to create results from purely verbal instructions.

Below is an example of the progression from confusing directions that are difficult to see clearly to understandable directions:

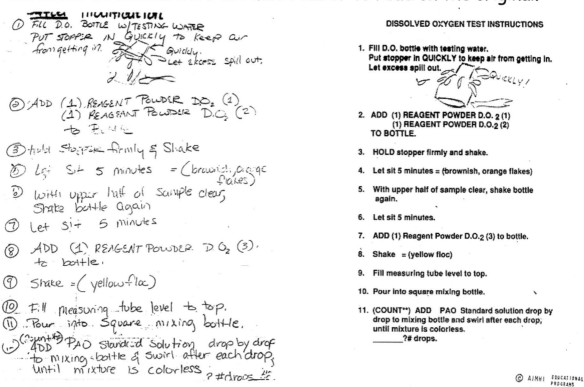

High Range Test Instructions

1. Fill the Dissolved Oxygen bottle (round bottle with glass stopper) with the water to be tested by allowing the water to overflow the bottle for two or three minutes. To avoid trapping air bubbles in the bottle incline the bottle slightly and insert the stopper with a quick thrust. This will force air bubbles out. If bubbles become trapped in the bottle in Steps 2 or 4 the sample should be discarded before repeating the test.

2. Use the clippers to open one Dissolved Oxygen 1 Reagent Powder Pillow and one Dissolved Oxygen 2 Reagent Powder. Add the contents of each of the pillows to the bottle. Stopper the bottle carefully to exclude air bubbles. Seal and stopper firmly; shake vigorously to mix. A flocculant (floc) precipitate will be formed. If oxygen is present in the sample the precipitate will be brownish orange in color. A small amount of powdered reagent may remain stuck to the bottom of the bottle. This will not affect the test results.

3. Allow the sample to stand until the floc has settled halfway in the bottle, leaving the upper half of the sample clear. Shake the bottle again. Again let it stand until the upper half of the sample is clear. Note the floc will not settle in samples with high concentrations of chloride, such as sea water. No interference with the test results will occur as long as the sample is allowed to stand for four or five minutes.

4. Use the clippers to open one Dissolved Oxygen 3 Reagent Powder Pillow. Remove the stopper from the bottle and add the contents of the pillow. Carefully restopper the bottle and shake to mix. The floc will dissolve and a yellow color will develop if oxygen is present.

5. Fill the plastic measuring tube level full of the sample prepared in Steps 1 through 4. Pour the sample into the square mixing bottle.

6. Add PAO Standard Solution drop by drop to the mixing bottle, swirling to mix after each drop. Hold the dropper vertically above the bottle and count each drop as it is added. Continue to add drops until the sample changes from yellow to colorless.

7. Each drop used to bring about the color change in Step 6 is equal to 1 mg/L of dissolved oxygen (DO).

Low Range Test Instructions

If the result of the Step 7 is very low (3 mg/L or less) it is advisable to

1. Use the prepared sample left from Step 4 in the High Range Test. Pour the level just reaches the mark (30 mL) on the bottle.

2. Add PAO Standard Solution drop by drop directly to the DO bottle. Cap the bottle constantly to mix while adding the titrant. Continue to add until yellow to colorless.

3. Each drop of PAO Standard Solution used to bring about the color change is dissolved oxygen.

REPLACEMENTS

Cat. No.	Description
981-99	Dissolved Oxygen 1 Reagent Powder Pillows
982-99	Dissolved Oxygen 2 Reagent Powder Pillows
987-99	Dissolved Oxygen 3 Reagent Powder Pillows
1079-37	Phenylarsine Oxide Standard Solution 0.0109N
1909-02	Bottle, Dissolved Oxygen, glass-stoppered
439-06	Bottle, mixing
968-00	Clippers
1909-01	Stopper, for dissolved oxygen bottle
438-00	Tube, measuring 5.83 mL
357-37	Copper Sulfate-Sulfamic Acid Solution APHA (not included
349-37	Starch Indicator Solution (not included in kit)
1949-00	Cylinder, graduated, 500 mL (not included in kit)
1864-41	Siphon (not included in kit)
7134-00	Tubing (not included in kit)

Method Dropping Bottle
Hach Company, 1982, 1983, 1985. All rights reserved.
MADE IN U.S.A.

Before

The above directions were not much easier to read on the original.

First rewrite:

① FILL D.O. BOTTLE w/ TESTING WATER PUT STOPPER IN QUICKLY to keep air from getting in. Quickly. Let excess spill out.

② ADD (1) REAGENT POWDER DO₂ (1) (1) REAGENT POWDER D.O₂ (2) to bottle.

③ Hold stopper firmly & shake

④ Let sit 5 minutes = (brownish, orange flakes)

⑥ With upper half of sample clear, shake bottle again

⑦ Let sit 5 minutes

⑧ ADD (1) REAGENT POWDER D.O₂ (3) to bottle.

⑨ Shake = (yellow floc)

⑩ Fill measuring tube level to top.

⑪ Pour into square mixing bottle.

⑫ (count**) ADD PAO standard solution drop by drop to mixing bottle & swirl after each drop, until mixture is colorless ? #drops __

Second and final rewrite:

DISSOLVED OXYGEN TEST INSTRUCTIONS

1. Fill D.O. bottle with testing water.
   Put stopper in QUICKLY to keep air from getting in.
   Let excess spill out. QUICKLY!

2. ADD (1) REAGENT POWDER D.O.₂ (1)
   (1) REAGENT POWDER D.O.₂ (2)
   TO BOTTLE.

3. HOLD stopper firmly and shake.

4. Let sit 5 minutes = (brownish, orange flakes)

5. With upper half of sample clear, shake bottle again.

6. Let sit 5 minutes.

7. ADD (1) Reagent Powder D.O.₂ (3) to bottle.

8. Shake = (yellow floc)

9. Fill measuring tube level to top.

10. Pour into square mixing bottle.

11. (COUNT**) ADD PAO Standard solution drop by drop to mixing bottle and swirl after each drop, until mixture is colorless.
    _____ ?# drops.

© AIMHI EDUCATIONAL PROGRAMS

CLEARLY DEFINE EXPECTATIONS

PROJECT:

U.S. History 1   Time period: 1600-1750
Development of the THIRTEEN English Colonies and Three Major Regions

These are virtually the same directions that you copied into your notebooks in class... but for anyone who was absent, or might need to check exactly what my expectations are, you now have this copy. In addition, library dates, class work period, and due dates are listed.

1.   This is a group project.

2.   There are three groups in each class. (New England, Middle, and Southern)

3.   There will be three library days initially: October 19th, 20th, 21st.

4.   There will be class work and organization in the room October 25, 1999.

> **Teacher clearly defines her expectations.**

5.   Each group will present a poster, travel brochure or Power Point presentation that covers the requirements. Your job is to teach the class about your region.

6.   Each group must have a minimum of 8 sources. (You may hand in the library cards.)

7.   Each group must complete and hand in the "library" organization sheet.

REQUIREMENTS (Check them off as you meet them.)

☐ Map with a minimum of 10 geographical features identified
☐ Government: What type colonies? (Corporate or character; royal; proprietary)
☐ Why were the colonies in your region founded? When and by whom?
☐ Religions and evidence of (or lack of) toleration
☐ Schools/Education
☐ Occupations and trade... How to make a living?
☐ Native Americans
☐ Climate and Crops
☐ Famous people
☐ Other: can include any interesting tidbits of information that you find

> **Checkboxes help students meet each requirement.**

DUE DATES
New England Colonies: Monday, November 8, 1999
Middle Colonies: Tuesday, November 9, 1999
Southern Colonies: Wednesday, November 10, 1999

PLEASE NOTE: Each individual is required to hand in a self-evaluation. Details will be furnished to you.
Also: If you are absent on your scheduled presentation date, you will be given an alternate assignment... no exceptions.

QUESTIONS???????? You need to ask!!

Contributed by Barbara Mee

USE POINTS FOR ACCOUNTABILITY AND MOTIVATION
NAME_____

WORLD HISTORY RESUME PROJECT

Late Nineteenth (1870's) to mid-Twentieth (1940's) Century Historical Figur

DUE DATE: _____

REQUIREMENTS: RESUME (one side of page only/typed or blue or black ink
A resume is used to help a person show how qualified he or she is for a part
position. In your résumé, you will BE the person you have researched and yo
following items:

PE/PP

_____ / 5 **Objective-** be creative- tell what position f

_____ / 15 **Work experience-** This lists jo

_____ / 15 **Accomplishments-** Describe the great things that you have done here:
Your paintings, novels, inventions, engineering feats,
Etc. Including dates.

_____ / 5 **Education-** Whether formal or informal, describe your education here,
beginning with the most advanced degree first.

_____ / 5 **Interests-** Include hobbies and other past times you enjoy.

_____ / 5 **Other-** This may include professional organizations you belong to, personal
information you would like to share, or perhaps a quote or some-
thing else you are well known for. You may discuss the impact of
what you have done. You may include a list of references also.

_____ / 10 **NEATNESS**
_____ / 15 **Bibliography Cards**
_____ / 15 **Formal Bibliography**
_____ / 90 **TOTAL POINTS**
_____   **Percentage Grade**

> Put point values on each part of an assignment.
>
> Your expectations will be clear and students will think twice before skipping parts.
>
> Rubrics can be used in the same manner.

Your "name" (topic you have chosen) must be prominently displayed on the project.
You should also include an *address and e-mail or telephone number.* Obviously, these may be
fictional. Be sure to *include your real name* here, too. Spelling, grammar, and punctuation are
all critical. There is a program on MSWord called Resume Wizard that may be used.

Point values for each section are listed above. Write your formal bibliography on a separate
sheet of paper, and tape your cards to the back of it.

Points earned = PE
Points possible = PP

PROVIDE LINES AND SPACE

Following is an **example of an assignment that is formatted in a way that is difficult** for students with reading issues, organizational problems, or difficulty focusing to process efficiently and accurately.

Simply **adapting the format so that it includes clear instructions** free of extra verbiage and adding lines to write the answers to the questions, allows the student to work on the goal of the assignment rather than be diverted by the difficulty the format presents.

ACTIVITY: SUSTAINABLE VS UNSUSTAINABLE ENVIRONMENT
PRE-ACTIVITY HOMEWORK ASSIGNMENT

For homework, each of you should find two articles. One article should explain one thing we can do to help make our environment sustainable, the other article should explain one thing that human beings are doing that is having a negative impact on the environment. As part of the assignment, complete the following questions on a separate sheet of paper.

You will be given several days to complete this assignment. It is important that you put a lot of effort into this assignment. The information you obtain on your own will be important to the success of your group when we use the information to complete a group activity in the near future.

1. Define the term sustainable.
2. Explain what you think a sustainable environment would look like.
3. Write an essay briefly describe the important points discussed in the article.
4. Most important: with the first article, describe why the activity being done helps make the environment sustainable. With the second article, describe why the activity being done is having a negative impact on the environment.

Consider how you might adapt the above assignment for different learning styles, personality types, multiple intelligences, and brain-based techniques.

Brainstorm with a colleague. List ideas here:

ADAPTED ASSIGNMENT EXAMPLE
(Note: Used Comic Sans MS Font & added lines and space)

"SUSTAINABLE VS UNSUSTAINABLE ENVIRONMENT"ACTIVITIES

Define, in your own words, the term SUSTAINABLE:

_____
_____
_____
_____

After sharing your definition with your group, write the definition of
SUSTAINABLE that the group has decided on:

_____
_____
_____
_____

Describe what you think a SUSTAINABLE ENVIRONMENT   would look like:

_____
_____
_____
_____

ARTICLE # 1: (Explains something we can do to help make our environment
sustainable.)

TITLE: _____
AUTHOR: _____
SOURCE: _____
SUMMARY OF ARTICLE: _____

_____
_____
_____

ARTICLE #2: (Explains something that human beings are doing that has a negative
impact on the environment.)

TITLE: _____
AUTHOR: _____
SOURCE: _____
SUMMARY OF ARTICLE: _____

_____
_____
_____

PROVIDE CHECKBOXES

Following is an example of a project description with and without checkboxes. From which would you prefer to work?

- -

Not Adapted

Constellation Project

Introduction: The sky is an evening's entertainment. It is free and there for the viewing on any clear night. The night sky is alive with meteors, the planets, stars, and a vast gallery of imaginary figures – the constellations.

Once you know some of the many myths associated with the stars and constellations, the night sky becomes a splendid picture book brimming with adventures of mythical heroes, maidens, and monsters. With just a little practice, you will soon learn to find your way among the stars.

On a clear night, you can see about 1,500 stars with the unaided eye. These stars range in brightness and color. 7-power binoculars will reveal a few thousand more stars than you can see with the unaided eye. Among the objects you can expect to see with binoculars are variable stars, couple stars and galaxies far and beyond our own. Knowledge of the constellations will help you locate them.

Directions: 1.Once you have been assigned a constellation, you will need to complete the following steps.

1. Look up the constellation in a book and draw the pattern of stars that make it up. Connect the star patterns with dashed lines. Please do this in black pen or pencil on plain white paper. You can even line up your pattern with a sketch of the imaginary figure it represents but this is not necessary. The engraving should be no larger than a third of the paper. It will be cut out and mounted on black construction paper when it is done.

2. Look up a myth surrounding your constellation. Summarize the story in pen on plain white paper. This will be mounted on the bottom two thirds of the black construction paper.

3. Identify the important stars in your drawing of the constellation and then describe each one by giving its magnitude, color temperature, and any other interesting information. In addition, identify how the star is classified; main sequence, white dwarf, or red giant.

After Adaptation

NAME_____PER_____DATE_____

CONSTELLATION PROJECT CHECKLIST

> ## CHECK OFF EACH ITEM AS YOU COMPLETE IT!

1. ☐ Look up the constellation in a book. (There are books in the library and the science class.)
2. ☐ Draw the pattern of the stars that make it up.

> A. Use plain white paper.
> B. Use BLACK ink or pencil.
> C. Make it no LARGER than 3 ½ "(height) X 8" (length).

3. ☐ Connect the star patterns with DASHED lines.
4. ☐ Cut out your constellations and mount it on BLACK construction paper at the TOP of the sheet.
5. ☐ Pierce PIN HOLES (not massive holes) through the stars.
6. ☐ Look up the myth about your constellation.
7. ☐ Write the story (myth) in YOUR OWN WORDS.
8. ☐ The final draft should be in PEN on plain WHITE PAPER.
9. ☐ State where the myth comes from.
10. ☐ Mount the myth BELOW your constellation on the black construction paper. (8 ½" X 11").
11. ☐ Identify the IMPORTANT stars in your drawing.
12. ☐ List these stars on the "IMPORTANT STAR CHART" (this is a special handout).
13. ☐ DESCRIBE AND RECORD in the chart, the important stars, by giving:

> A. Magnitude
> B. Color
> C. Temperature
> D. Other interesting facts
> E. Classification (white dwarf, red giant, etc)

Successful Inclusion Strategies

CONSTELLATIONS

STEP 1

Constellations are groupings of stars. They are based upon the imagination of man. Ancient peoples gazed in wonder at the night sky. They noticed that certain stars seemed to form patterns. Ancient people saw these patterns as earthly things or as characters in their mythology. They gave them names such as Orion, Leo, Capricornus, and Ursa Major.

Stars in constellations are not related to each other scientifically. They are usually brighter and closer to the earth than most other stars.

Recognizing constellations, however, is important. They help astronomers pinpoint the locations of certain stars, nebulae, and galaxies. Ship captains, aircraft navigators, astronauts, desert caravans, and many other travelers have used them. Constellations and many of their stars are used to determine directions and one's location on earth.

People in the northern hemisphere look up at a different sky than those in the southern hemisphere. We use different constellations, nebulae, and galaxies than they do. Standing straight above the north geographical pole is the pole star. It is called Polaris. The earth is rotating directly under Polaris. Because of this, all northern constellations seem to revolve around Polaris once a day. That is why the Big Dipper may be found in a different location during the same night.

Constellations in the northern hemisphere close to the pole star are called circumpolar constellations. The most well known ones are Ursa Major, Ursa Minor, Cepheus, Draco, and Cassiopeia. They are above the horizon all during the year.

Step II

Here you will find a word search:

F U I O M H T R M V F D W L L I O P J D F
A S D F G H J K I U Y N M L P 4E W D D S
F U I O M H T R M V F D W L L I O P J D F
A S D F G H J K I U Y N M L P 4E W D D S
F U I O M H T R M V F D W L L I O P J D F
A S D F G H J K I U Y N M L P 4E W D D S
F U I O M H T R M V F D W L L I O P J D F
A S D F G H J K I U Y N M L P 4E W D D S

STEP 3

Answer an essay question on the following lines

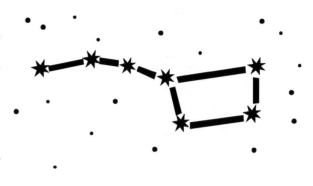

FINDING THE POLE STAR

Step 3
This section of the worksheet is a fill in section that is very small with very small spaces to answer the questions.

This is the first question and the answer goes here _____.
And that's all the room that you get.
This is the second question and that's all the room that you get because the answer goes here _____.
This is the _____ question and the answer goes here _____. And that's all the room that you get.
This is the fourth question and the _____ goes here _____. And that's all the room that you get.
This is the fifth question and the answer goes here _____.
And that's all the _____ that you get.
This is the sixth question and the answer goes here _____.
And that's all the room that you get.
Etc.
This is the first question and the answer goes here _____.
And that's all the room that you get.
This is the second question and that's all the room that you get because the answer goes here _____.
This is the _____ question and the answer goes here _____. And that's all the room that you get.
This is the fourth question and the _____ goes here _____. And that's all the room that you get.
This is the fifth question and the answer goes here _____.
And that's all the _____ that you get.
This is the sixth question and the answer goes here _____.
And that's all the room that you get.
Etc.

_____

_____

This is NOT a real worksheet. This is a "visual" example. The word search is not real.

CONSTELLATIONS

STEP 1

Constellations are groupings of stars. They are based upon the imagination of man. Ancient peoples gazed in wonder at the night sky. They noticed that certain stars seemed to form patterns. Ancient people saw these patterns as earthly things or as characters in their mythology. They gave them names such as Orion, Leo, Capricornus, and Ursa Major.

Stars in constellations are not related to each other scientifically. They are usually brighter and closer to the earth than most other stars.

Recognizing constellations, however, is important. They help astronomers pinpoint the locations of certain stars, nebulae, and galaxies. Ship captains, aircraft navigators, astronauts, desert caravans, and many other travelers have used them. Constellations and many of their stars are used to determine directions and one's location on earth.

People in the northern hemisphere look up at a different sky than those in the southern hemisphere. We use different constellations, nebulae, and galaxies than they do. Standing straight above the north geographical pole is the pole star. It is called Polaris. The earth is rotating directly under Polaris. Because of this, all northern constellations seem to revolve around Polaris once a day. That is why the Big Dipper may be found in a different location during the same night.

Constellations in the northern hemisphere close to the pole star are called circumpolar constellations. The most well known ones are Ursa Major, Ursa Minor, Cepheus, Draco, and Cassiopeia. They are above the horizon all during the year.

ADAPTATION OF TRADITIONAL WORLD HISTORY REPORT: PROVIDE CHOICE

ASSIGNMENT: NEWS PROJECT   DUE DATE_____

CHOOSE ONE: Newspaper Reporter
                       Radio Commentator
                       TV Commentator

NEWSPAPER REPORTER: You are a reporter who has been given a special project. The time period is _____. You must choose your own topic (be specific) and write a feature article. As with any newspaper, the article must be well written or the editor will not accept it, and you will not be paid (with a grade). You will be given one chance to rewrite it for credit.
It must be historically accurate and interesting to read. You must, in your article, establish why the event is important or will be important to historians and other people in the future.

BASIC SET UP:

☐	a) Minimum of 1 full written page on stand.
☐	b) Must be set up to look like an actual newspaper article.
☐	c) Final copy in ink or typed.

REQUIREMENTS	DATE DUE
☐ Topic approved	
☐ Research completed	
☐ Final copy due	

RADIO OR TV COMMENTATOR: You are a radio news reporter (or TV reporter) who has been given a special project. The time period is _____. You must choose your own topic (be specific) and make a recorded audio (or video) tape of the topic. As with any special radio (or TV) report, your taped feature must be interesting and presented in a professional radio (or TV) manner. As always, the editor must approve the taped program or you will not be paid (with a grade). A one-page fact sheet must be presented with your recording. You will be given one chance to re-tape your news feature and re-write your fact sheet. It must be historically accurate and interesting to hear (or watch). You must, in your recordings, establish why the event is important or will be important to the historians and other people in the future.

BASIC SET UP:

☐	a) 1 page fact sheet must be handed in with the tape.
☐	b) News show must be presented like an actual radio (TV) news show.
☐	c) Final copy in ink or typed.

REQUIREMENTS	DATE DUE
☐ Topic approved	
☐ Research completed	
☐ Final copy due	

Are you tired of seeing math problems all jumbled up on an unlined piece of paper? Does it cause students with special and organizational difficulties to make mistakes because numbers and equations are not lined up properly? Does it make correcting difficult? Here's a simple solution!

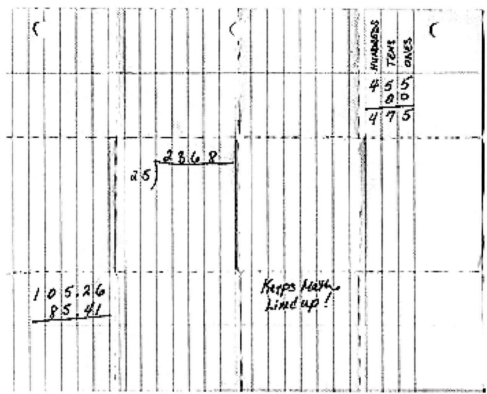

Keep math lined up!
Turn standard lined paper sideways.
Grid paper also works very well. Make your own grid paper with enlarged grids.

USING GRIDS AND SPACE TO TEACH MATH

Name_____Date_____

Corporate Income Tax

Taxable income is the portion of your company's gross income that remains after normal business expenses are deducted. The structure of federal corporate income taxes is illustrated.

TAXABLE INCOME = ANNUAL GROSS INCOME – DEDUCTIONS

Refer to the table on page 532 (21-1) of your textbook for federal corporate income tax rates.

Corporation	Kenmare	Chen Wok	S J Wells	PDF
Annual Gross Income	$216,750.00	$116,418.00	$67,800.00	$217,400.00
Deductions	$98,415.00	$51,420.00	$24,950.00	$125,350.00
Taxable Income				
Total Tax				

5. Dragon Manufacturing Company has these business expenses for the year:

Wages	$ 516,450.00	Property taxes	$174,196.00
Rent	$ 48,000.00	Depreciation	$ 38,750.00
Utilities	$ 13,960.00	Other deductions	$ 14,614.90
Interest	$ 6,247.85		

Dragon has gross income of $1,826,000 for the year.
What is the total of Dragon's business expenses?   _____

What is Dragon's **taxable income**?   _____

What is Dragon's federal corporate income tax for the year?   _____

6. Dr. S. Cleary formed a medical corporation. The corporation had these business expenses for the year:

Wages	$56,500.00	Property Taxes	$ 4,749.00
Utilities	$ 7,840.00	Depreciation	$14,9916.50
Interest	$ 6,000.00	Other deductions	$ 3,500.00

The corporate's gross income for the year was $154,850.
What is the federal corporate income tax for the year?   _____

7. Your business had a gross income of $874,600.00 for the year. You deducted the following business expenses from the gross income:

Wages	$574,600.00	Interest	$ 9,800.00
Utilities	$ 10,630.00	Depreciation	$20,294.00
Rent	$ 48,000.00	Other deductions	$11,430.00

What is the total for business expenses?   _____

What was the **taxable income**?   _____

What was the federal corporate income tax for the year?   _____

Students color code the worksheet with highlighters.

Annual Gross Income	Total Deductions	Taxable Income	Tax amount from Chart (if any)	Of The Amount Over (from Chart)
$216,750	$98,415			
$116,418	$51,429			
$67,800	$24,950			
#5) $1,826,000				
#6)				
#7)				

Match color coding here:

Annual Gross Income is Yellow, Total Deductions is light blue, and Taxable Income is Pink.

The worksheet on the previous page did not come ready made with the grid presented here. Paul simply created a grid and had students highlight key terms on the worksheet. Then those terms were highlighted to match on this grid. Students are more successful doing the math because of the added structure and format.

Dollar Amount Over	Percent (from Chart)	Tax Amount	Tax Total

Idea contributed by Paul Favreau, Manchester, NH

HALF-SHEET THEORY[1]

The half-sheet theory is very simple. Instead of putting homework problems on one side of one sheet of paper, put them on both sides of a half sheet of paper. Psychologically, students think they are only getting a half sheet of homework. Then if they complain about homework, you can say, "Ah, it's just a half sheet. Come on, you can do a half sheet of homework!"

It's a little more work to run problems on both sides of a paper and cut it down the middle, but, according to Annette Gorgoglione, a high school math teacher, it works!

Reduce to lowest terms

$\frac{10}{40}$ =	$\frac{8}{20}$ =	$\frac{40}{50}$ =	$\frac{9}{12}$ =	$\frac{5}{20}$ =
$\frac{20}{25}$ =	$\frac{4}{10}$ =	$\frac{4}{40}$ =	$\frac{10}{20}$ =	$\frac{4}{20}$ =
$\frac{2}{6}$ =	$\frac{15}{20}$ =	$\frac{3}{15}$ =	$\frac{12}{15}$ =	$\frac{20}{30}$ =
$\frac{30}{40}$ =	$\frac{6}{10}$ =	$\frac{3}{9}$ =	$\frac{2}{20}$ =	$\frac{20}{50}$ =
$\frac{3}{30}$ =	$\frac{6}{8}$ =	$\frac{6}{15}$ =	$\frac{3}{12}$ =	$\frac{12}{20}$ =
$\frac{4}{8}$ =	$\frac{2}{10}$ =	$\frac{10}{25}$ =	$\frac{2}{8}$ =	$\frac{5}{10}$ =
$\frac{10}{15}$ =	$\frac{15}{25}$ =	$\frac{4}{6}$ =	$\frac{8}{12}$ =	$\frac{5}{50}$ =
$\frac{8}{10}$ =	$\frac{10}{50}$ =	$\frac{3}{6}$ =	$\frac{10}{30}$ =	$\frac{6}{9}$ =

---

[1] Idea contributed by Annette Gorgoglione, Londonderry High School, Londonderry, NH

Interventions and Adaptations for Students with AD(H)D

Robert daydreamed so much that he was put out of school. Frank went into such trancelike dreams that one had to shout at him to bring him back. Equally problematic were Sam's restlessness and verbal diatribes. Virginia, too, demonstrated a tendency to talk on and on. Thomas experienced school problems, in part because of his high energy. Nick's tendency to act without thinking caused him to have several scrapes with death and near-tragedies, such as plunging to the earth from the roof of a barn, clutching an umbrella. In these examples we can see how the concentration, high energy, and unique ways of thinking and behaving that were exemplified by Robert Frost, Frank Lloyd Wright, Samuel Taylor Coleridge, Virginia Woolf, Thomas Edison, and Nikola Tesla resulted in school problems, dark diagnoses, or worse. These are examples of creative individuals whose behavior could also be interpreted as the inattention, impulsivity, and hyperactivity of Attention Deficit Hyperactivity Disorder.

--Bonnie Cramond, Ph.D., The University of Georgia, March 1995,
http://borntoexplore.org/adhd.htm

TIPS TO HELP STUDENTS HAVING DIFFICULTY WITH ATTENTION AND DISTRACTIBILITY

- Make use of **non-verbal signals** to cue student before transitions, or to stop all activity and focus on the teacher.
- Assign students **Task Buddie**s to help keep partner on task.
- Seat students near the center of instruction.
- Seat distractible students surrounded by well-focused students.
- Use physical proximity to help cue student to return to task.
- Allow **quiet fidget toys, doodling, or mandalas** to help students focus.
- Clearly define expectations.
- **Vary tone of voice** when presenting to students. (If you can pull off a dramatic flair, it works well.)
- **Provide study carrels or partitions** to reduce visual distractions during seatwork or test-taking as appropriate. (This should be a student choice not a punishment.)
- **Provide sound reducing headsets** for students to minimize auditory distractions.
- When possible, engage students in unstructured, creative challenges.
- **Color or highlight directions and important words** on the assignment.
- During silent reading, consider allowing students to **sit on the floor** if they ask. Some students become amazingly focused when they carve out their own space on the floor or in a corner in the classroom.
- Allow students to ask buddies for clarification on seatwork.
- Significantly increase opportunities for active student involvement in the lesson and utilize questioning techniques that engage all students.
- Consider allowing ADHD students to "tutor" other students in areas of strength. This often brings out focused, caring behavior and encourages self-esteem.

Adaptations for Auditory Processing Difficulties

Follow the suggestions for ADD, ADHD. Students with auditory processing difficulties often exhibit the same or similar behaviors as students with ADHD. A speech therapist whose expertise was Central Auditory Processing Disorder (she had CAPD) shared that many students diagnosed with ADHD were actually CAPD, but rarely tested for it. Some vision difficulties also mimic ADHD.

- Supplement verbal presentation with **visuals, color, graphics, and demonstrations.**
- **Allow time** for processing information – **Slow down.**
- Increase amount of eye contact with students.
- **Follow the ten-second rul**e before calling on students to respond to a question.
- Provide directions in **written as well as verbal** form.
- If spelling is an issue, **allow a spell checker or text editor** to complete writing assignments.
- Keep **background noise in the classroom to a minimum** when lecturing or presenting information to the whole class. *Students with CAPD cannot process what they hear* when there is *background noise.* If possible, get a Sound Screen.
- **Monitor frequently** for student understanding.
- Write major points or content **outline on the board.**
- Offer many choices that **involve creative expression**.
- Provide an **outline or overview** of the lesson.
- Relate information to students' experience and background information.
- **Summarize key points** and let students know what is important for them to remember.

A SOLUTION FOR STUDENTS WHO ROCK BACK AND FIDGET IN THEIR SEATS

Students who tip back on two legs of their chairs in class often are stimulating their brain with a rocking, vestibular-activating motion. They are trying to wake up their (brain's) vestibular system. While it is an unsafe activity, it happens to be good for the brain.

What can teachers do?
1. Give students activities that let them move safely more often like role-plays, skits, and stretching.

2. Have students who chronically rock balance on a rocking board while doing worksheets on a podium. It helps them to concentrate and keeps them from fidgeting.

3. Build a small under desk version of a rocking board. Students sit at their desks with their feet on a rocking board underneath and it keeps them from rocking back in their chairs.

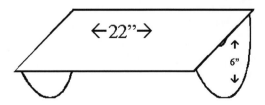

Considerations for Students in the Autistic Spectrum

Most of the strategies for students with AD(H)D and Auditory Processing Difficulties apply for students in the Autistic Spectrum. Following are some additional and specific considerations.

Communicating to the Student
- Be concrete and specific. Avoid using vague terms like later, maybe, "why did you do that?"
- Avoid idioms, double meanings, and sarcasm.
- Use gestures, modeling, and demonstrations with verbalization.
- Specifically engage attention visually, verbally, or physically.
- Use picture cues to communicate when possible.

Structure the Environment and Class Routine
- If necessary for understanding, break tasks down into smaller steps.
- Provide accurate, prior information about change and expectations. Minimize transitions.
- Offer consistent daily routine.
- Avoid surprises, prepare thoroughly and in advance for special activities, altered schedules, or other changes, regardless of how minimal.
- Talk through stressful situations or remove him/her from the stressful situation.
- Allow for a 'safe space' in the building for student to retreat to when necessary.
- Reduce distractions and sensory overloads: Noise, vision, smell.
- Provide a designated work area. This could be a place mat on a desk.
- Label areas for materials the student will access or store.
- Provided a visually coded organization system for materials and notebooks.
- Post checklists and reminder cards to keep student on task and organized.
- Let student go a little earlier or later than the bell. Halls are a source of difficulty.
- Teach use of timer or other visual cues to manage behavior.

Presentation of Material
- Use visual in teaching and learning materials
- Use graphic organizers, charts, diagrams, and computer video clips.

Structured Teaching--The TEACCH approach

Structured teaching is an important priority because of the TEACCH research and experience that structure fits the "culture of autism" more effectively than any other techniques we have observed. Organizing the physical environment, developing schedules and work systems, making expectations clear and explicit, and using visual materials have been effective ways of developing skills and allowing people with autism to use these skills independently of direct adult prompting and cueing. These priorities are especially important for students with autism who are frequently held back by their inability to work independently in a variety of situations. Structured teaching says nothing about where people with autism should be educated; this is a decision based on the skills and needs of each individual student.

For more information go to http://www.teacch.com

Strategies That Enhance Memorization and Recall

MIND MAPPING/GRAPHIC ROADMAPS/VISUAL ORGANIZERS

I started using mind mapping after reading *I Can See You Naked: a Fearless Guide to Making Great Presentations* by Ron Hoff (1988). My first presentation was drawn out like a colorful board game with a route to follow, arrows, and picture images of what I was going to do. I remember thinking how much easier it was to use than index cards with a text script written on them. It also was much less restricting. I did not feel tied to reading the cards. Rather, I looked at the picture and went from memory. It saved me from the plight of many presenters: that of being tied to a script.

The technique worked so well for me that I started expanding the idea into my teaching efforts. **As I read selections from English texts to my students, I drew the events out on paper in map and graphic format.** I would often interject silly ditties and exclamations of passion into the effort to make what I was reading to them stick out in their memory. Given my students were at the 'cool' age of 'teen' they would often look at me and say, "you are crazy!' My pat answer was always, "Yes, I am, but you'll remember this because of it". Moreover, they did.

Students learn and remember mind maps better if they create them out of their own mental images and patterns. See examples below.

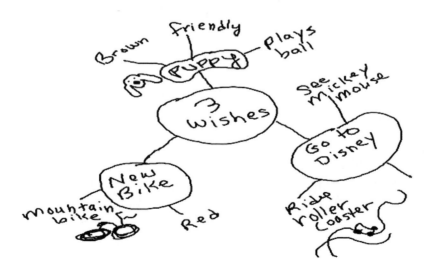

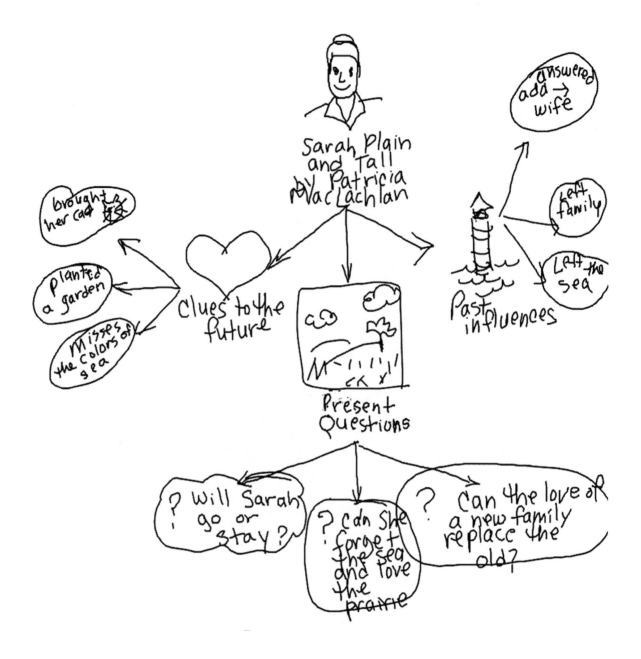

When students make spelling errors at this phase of the creative process, note them, but let them go. Correcting students' spelling while they are creating will cause them to clutter their working memory with rules and not allow enough "space" for coming up with ideas. So, correct the difference between 'add' and 'ad' later.

MEMORY MODELS

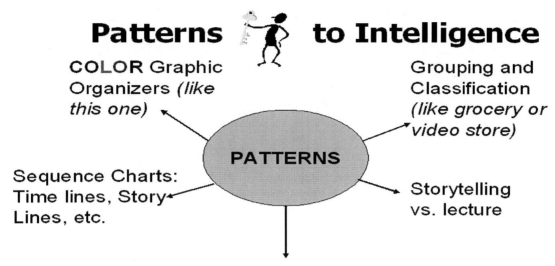

Patterns to Intelligence

COLOR Graphic Organizers *(like this one)*

Grouping and Classification *(like grocery or video store)*

PATTERNS

Sequence Charts: Time lines, Story Lines, etc.

Storytelling vs. lecture

Ask kids to find patterns: *cause and effect*, problem and solution, intense drama and down time.

A memory model provides a three-dimensional model for your memory to work with.[1] I first saw memory models used in a methods workshop on teaching a unit on the ocean. The presenter had physical objects as symbolic representation of ocean processes. It was fascinating.

While teaching a unit on the respiratory system, I use a memory model to introduce the vocabulary for the unit. Again, some students, believing that such things were childish (well, we had to wean them away from such things in upper elementary and middle school to prepare them for being big kids in high school, right?) thought I was crazy. So be it. My attitude is if it helps them learn, I do not care if they think I am nuts. Memory models are wonderfully useful, time consuming to prepare (the first time) but worth it if your goal is increased retention.

RESPIRATORY SYSTEM MEMORY MODEL:

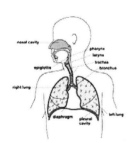  

Flap inside = epiglottis
Filter = cilia
Canister = lung

Minimaze = Alveoli (demonstrating the exchange of O^2 and CO^2

Diagram used to teach the respiratory system

Corrugated hose = trachea
Ribbing in hose = cartilage

 Sponge = Lung tissue

Line up 'models' in the order they would be in the respiratory system.

---

[1] Hoff, Ron. (1988) *I Can See You Naked: A fearless Guide to Making Great Presentations* Kansas City, MO: Andrews and McMeel.

MNEMONIC DEVICES [2]

Mnemonic: n. A device, such as a formula or rhyme, used as an aid in remembering.

Mnemonics, or the science or art of aiding memory, is an ancient concept. Many people rely on mnemonic devices to help remember what they have learned or need to recall, from grocery lists to people's names to kings and queens or the presidents. What works for one person may not work for another. The following five memory devices help to improve retention of information.

Some examples of mnemonics:
- I AM A PERSON: The four Oceans (Indian, Arctic, Atlantic, and Pacific).
- HOMES: Huron, Ontario, Michigan, Erie, and Superior: the Great Lakes in North America.

The best are those made up by the student, as they are meaningful to him/her.

ASSOCIATIONS

Developing associations is a familiar strategy used to recall information by connecting it to other, more familiar pieces of information. For example, memorizing a sequence of seemingly random digits is easy when that number series is your birth date or street address. Developing associations is also a helpful way to remember new information.

RHYMING

Rhymes and jingles are powerful memory devices. Just think how often you have used the rhyme, "Thirty days has September. . ." to recall the number of days within a month.

To use the Rhyme Technique all you have to do is make up a rhyme to remember what you want to remember! It's fun! If you are musically inclined, you can even make up whole songs to help you remember long pieces of important information.

Examples:
30 days has September
April, June, and November

In 1492, Columbus sailed the ocean blue.

In 1903, the Wright brothers flew free.
First successful flight

I before E except after C
And when saying "A" as in Neighbor or Weigh
And weird is weird.

---

[2] Adapted from the work of Michael DiSpezio, author of *Critical Thinking Puzzles* (Sterling, 1996) for Scientific American Frontiers. <http://www.pbs.org/saf/4_class/45_pguides/pguide_703/4573_trufalse.html>.

CHUNKING

When reciting a telephone or Social Security number, most people are apt to speak it in three chunks. For example, the first and second chunks of a phone number consist of three digits and the third chunk contains four digits. Chunking the numbers makes a meaningless series easier to remember. Can you think of other series of numbers that are frequently chunked?

800-566-3712

Chunking is also an excellent strategy for remembering how to spell words.
An example of chunking follows:

man EU ver

Other examples of chunked spelling words:

```
ALBU  QUER  QUE
RE  NUMER  ATION
PENN  SYLVAN  IA
CZ  ECHO  SLO  VAKIA
LEU  KE  MIA
FRE  NET  IC
RECE  IVE
```

ACRONYMS

An acronym is a word formed from the initial letter or letters of each of the parts of a name or organization. For example, the acronym **LASER** stands for **L**ight **A**mplification by **S**timulated **E**mission of **R**adiation. Some other familiar acronyms are **RADAR**, **R**EM sleep, SCUBA, SONAR, NASA, **Z**IP code, etc. You can also make up acronyms to help you remember information. Think of an acronym as a "fun" word or phrase in which each letter stands for the first letter of the item to be recalled.

ACROSTICS

An acrostic is a memory strategy similar to an acronym, but it takes the first letters of a series of words, lines, or verses to form a memorable phrase. Sometimes the phrase is nonsense, which may help you remember it! Here are two: **K**ing **P**hilip **C**ame **O**ver **F**or **G**reat **S**paghetti or **K**ings **P**lay **C**ards **O**n **F**at **G**reen **S**tools. Each acrostic stands for the biological classification hierarchy (**K**ingdom, **P**hylum, **C**lass, **O**rder, **F**amily, **G**enus, and **S**pecies).

STRATEGY TO REMEMBER SEQUENCES

Use adding machine tape to create a visual storyline, time line, or sequence to be memorized.

Instructions:
As your child is reading a textbook or story, he or she draws pictures of the important information (characters, historical figures, places, events, etc.) in the order that he or she reads the information on adding machine tape.

For example, when you read about how the Lakota used directions, you draw a picture of it on the tape. Next the chapter describes what types of information was recorded such as position of the sun, of the moon, neighbor sites, etc. Draw and label that information in the same sequence/order that it is listed or described in the textbook. See the following examples.

Now, the student has a "time line or story line" in sequential order of the events in the textbook or story. This visual memory tool will help him/her to remember the information in the order that it "happened".

COLOR AND MEMORY

Simply put, we remember what we see in color better than what we see in black and white. According to Eric Jensen in *Brain-Based Learning* (1996), we remember colors first and content next. Colors affect us on physiological and psychological levels.

- Use colored handouts
- Add color to overheads
- Print notes and alternate two colors for each individual point.
- Hang colorful posters to reinforce concepts being taught.
- Provide colorful visuals.

According to the research, color communicates more effectively than black and white. How much more effectively? Here's what the research says:

- Color visuals increase willingness to read by up to 80 percent.[3]
- Using color can increase motivation and participation by up to 80 percent.[3]
- Color enhances learning and improves retention by more than 75 percent.[4]
- Color accounts for 60 percent of the acceptance or rejection of an object and is a critical factor in the success of any visual experience. [5]

The Meaning of Color

- Red - An engaging and emotive color, which can stimulate hunger or excite and disturb the individual.
- Yellow - The first color distinguished by the brain.
- Blue - Calms a tense person and increases feelings of well-being.
- Green - A calming color, like blue.
- Brown - Promotes a sense of security and relaxation and reduces fatigue.

DRAW IT SO YOU'LL KNOW IT

- Teach 10 minutes
- Stop for 3 minutes (Use a timer)
- Instruct students to draw a picture of what you have taught them in the last ten minutes!

---

[3] *The Persuasive Properties of Color*, Ronald E. Green; Marketing Communications, October 1984.
[4] Loyola University School of Business, Chicago, IL., as reported in Hewlett-Packard's Advisor, June 1999; <http://www.hpadvisor.com>
[5] *The Power of Color*, Dr. Morton Walker; Avery Publishing Group; 1991.

When students are reading or reviewing previously read material:

- Have students draw pictures of what they are reading.
- Have them illustrate their notes with drawings that represent what is in the notes.

This drawing is actually done in color markers.
All pictures used in this handbook were originally done in color.

MAKE IT MEANINGFUL

BRING EMOTION INTO THE LESSON

We remember things that evoke our emotion. Advertisers use this knowledge effectively. When we can bring drama into the classroom, we will see increased learning. I will never forget the Western Civilization professor that I had in college and the excitement and passion she demonstrated for her subject. I hated history all through high school. Suddenly, I found myself enjoying a history class. Between my use of mnemonics and the teacher's drama, enthusiasm, and ability to relate what she taught to the real world including our future, I learned and loved it! Ms. Civitello, Thanks!

- Make it a story.
- Read with dramatization.
- Use a gripping picture.

Whenever possible, introduce concepts with pictures that evoke emotions. Many times, we focus on the printed word in texts and make minimal use of the photos. Artwork and drama reach the heart. Use it whenever possible to hook your students into the lesson.

Note: Use Photos as Tools for Brain Based Learning and Multiple Intelligences

"Students are more invested in what they are learning if they can apply it to their lives," explains, George Jackman, a high school industrial arts teacher. "Basically, I video the daily happenings, go to the computer desk top publishing station, pick those shots that best demonstrate concepts and words, then build a page."

"To insure that the students have extended practice opportunities with this information, I create a crossword (with built in prompts and cues!) that they do for homework. Through this process, students become familiar with practices and concepts. Because the pictures are current, (and images of themselves) kids see the exercise as "real" and of "quality"; something worth doing."

George states with conviction, "I know this is very empowering!

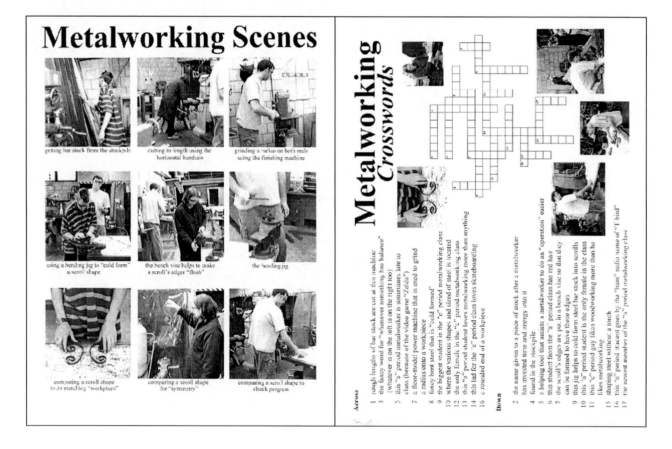

---

[6] Contributed by George Jackman, Londonderry High School, Londonderry, NH.

WHO AM I? : INTRODUCTION OR REVIEW

Materials:
- Index Cards or Card Stock (this can be run through most printers or copiers)
- Nametag pouches with the elastic cords to wear like a necklace.
- Source of pictures or a FEW words in print.

Instructions
- Make or buy cards that have a picture or name of a person, place, animal, or thing from the unit you are studying on one side of the card.
- Make them no wider than a nametag and no taller than 4 inches.
- Use cardstock and/or laminate the pieces for longevity and functionality. (They do not work well if the paper is so limp it flops over in the pouch).
- Warn each student about the consequences of snapping the elastic chords around another student's neck. Even if you remember to do this, you might have one lively child decide to snap one of the pouches.
- Students put the pouches around their necks.
- THEN so they cannot see you, put or have students put a card representing their identity in the pouch so that everyone else can see it.
- The student's goal is to guess his/her identity by going around the room and asking questions to investigate who he/she is.
- The student may ask ONLY YES or NO questions. Those answering questions must answer only YES or NO.
- The game is over when all students have guessed their identity, or you call time.

POSSIBLE TOPICS

- _____
- _____
- _____
- _____
- _____
- _____
- _____

Name Tag Pouch available at any office supply store to hold "player identity".

The Leaning Tower of Pisa

This activity makes learning meaningful by attaching new information to previous knowledge.

ZIP AROUND

Zip Around: Review
Zip Around is a great "quick" review game. Use vocabulary, key facts, concepts, people and dates, etc. First, make up the cards carefully following the instructions on the diagram below. If you are using questions and answers rather than words and definitions, Word becomes Fact and Definition becomes Answer.

If set up correctly, the person who starts the zip around will end the zip around. In order to achieve this "correctness" do not let yourself be interrupted while making the cards!

Once the cards are made, pass one to each of the players in the class. Ideally, each student will have one card. Keep one card for yourself and start the zipping around by reading the question or word on your card. (Remember the answer on the other side of your card is the answer to the last item that will be asked.)

The student with the answer calls out the answer by reading off the card then turns the card over and asks the NEXT question. Moreover, the game continues until all the cards have been answered and the game has zipped around the room and back to you.

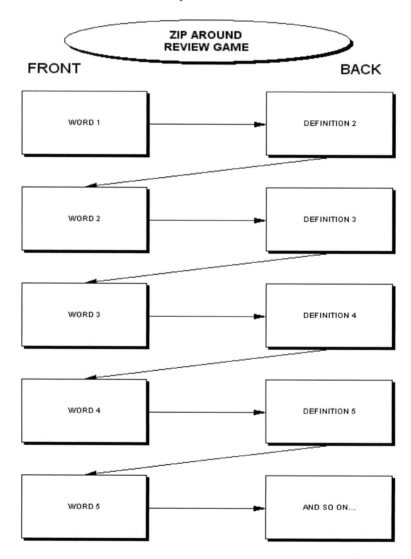

THREE CARD MATCH: REVIEW

Materials
- Index Cards
  - Choose three of the following card colors: pink, green, blue, yellow, or white.
  - If you only have white cards or white paper, color-code the cards. For example:
    - Put a yellow dot or stripe on the word cards.
    - Put a green dot or stripe on the picture cards.
    - Put a pink dot or stripe on the definition cards…and so on and so forth.
- Pictures
  - Of the item being reviewed
  - Or related to the concept being reviewed
  - Or mnemonic pictures to form an association

Instructions
1. Break down what they have to memorize into three related concepts, facts, pictures, meanings, etc.
2. Each card should contain one 'item'. (See example below)

3. Label the back of each card in a set with a number so children can turn the card over and self-correct.

For example:
The word elephant, the picture of the elephant and the definition of the elephant would all be numbered #1 on the back.

The word zebra, the picture of the zebra and the definition of the zebra would all be numbered #2, etc.

Options for use:

- Students can match the cards on their own as a review in the resource room or classroom. If they have their own sets, they may use them at home to study.

- Students can pair up to match the cards. This is an excellent peer tutoring activity.

Visual Or Mnemonic	Word	Definition
	Folium of Descartes	x^3 + y^3 == 3x*y
 BEETLES	coleoptera	Wings meet in a straight line, bottom wings are membranous, top wings form a hard cover.
 BUTTERFLIES AND MOTHS	lepidoptera	Wings are membranous and covered with scales.
 GRASSHOPPERS, CRICKETS & ROACHES	orthoptera	Wings are thin and veined. One pair of legs is more muscular.

Option 1:
Use phonics rules to determine which letters should be in a **stand-out color**.

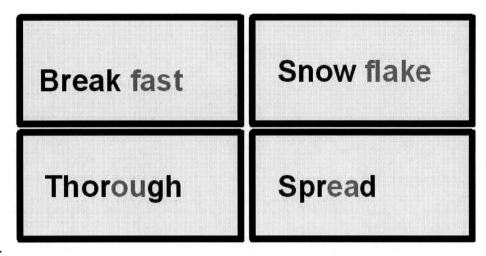

Option 2:
Pre-test
Use pre-test errors to determine which letters should be in a **stand-out color**.
Theory: Make the corrected mistake in spelling stand out so that the mistake is not repeated.

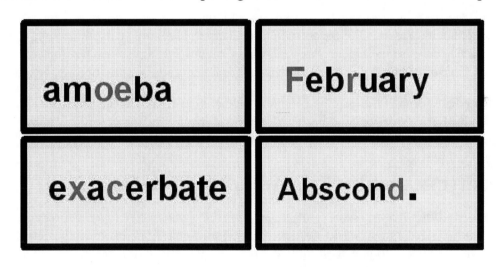

1.   Whenever possible, add clip art pictures to 'visualize' the word.
2.   Use bright color markers with good contrast to differentiate.
3.   Add any other symbols, sound cues, etc. to make the spelling word more memorable.
4.   PRINT the words on INDEX CARDS.
5.   Practice by running through the cards 2-3 times each day for the four days before the spelling test. Put aside the cards that need more study. Cards that can be spelled quickly can be pulled out of the daily second and third run.

Good luck! You should see a significant improvement in spelling test grades.

8

Grading

General Considerations

Grading special needs students in the regular classroom, especially at the high school level, is a problematic issue. The many opinions, points of view, and philosophies on the subject are often strongly held and emotionally laden. This is a tough one. The key is to find a method of grading in the inclusive classroom that is comfortable for you, the teacher, and fair for _all_ the students.

Standardized tests, most ready-made textbook tests, and many teacher-made pencil and paper tests seldom provide a fair assessment of the special needs learner. In all my years of teaching experience, I have rarely seen special needs students test well. I have often seen students do well on all coursework except tests. I have also seen students go down an entire letter grade because of a final exam.

If students can demonstrate understanding and knowledge in every other aspect of the class except tests, what do the tests prove? Standardized and traditional pencil and paper tests are a better indicator of short-term memory capability than acquisition of knowledge, comprehension of material, and application of knowledge.

OPTIONS TO TRADITIONAL GRADING SYSTEMS

- **Contract grading** often provides _clear expectations and achievable chunks_ for students. The student knows what is needed to acquire a grade and can work towards that goal. Often, students are clueless as to how their individual pieces of work figure into the final "grade." A contract provides a clear structure for students to work within.

- **Provide a structure where effort, behavior, preparedness, and prompt attendance are rewarded.** These traits are important in the workplace and should be reinforced in school. I give students 5 points/day based on these factors. It averages out to 20% of their grades. I would tell my students that if they did all their class work and home work to the best of their ability (50% of their grade); they could not fail my class even if they were horrible test takers. This system worked for most of my students. They all knew they could earn a minimum of a *C* no matter how badly they did on tests. _See Point Chart at the end of this chapter._

- **Use a variety of assessment tools** so that all learning styles are accommodated. The assessment tools used have a major impact on the grade earned. Even at the college level, a variety of assessment tools and methods are often used. The argument that pencil and paper testing prepares students for college is not accurate.

WHAT CONSTITUTES A LOWERED GRADE?[1]

Here is a good rule of thumb to follow based on current research and litigation.
If a student is receiving adaptations:
- He or she should be evaluated and graded similar to that of the general student population.
- The adaptations do not need to be indicated on the report card.

Adaptations are a civil rights issue.

If a student is receiving significant curriculum modifications
(curriculum content is reduced >33%), then:
- Pass/fail or credit/no-credit might be used on the report card.
- The school may change the course # for that student to indicate a different curriculum while in the general classroom *if that course option is available to the general population*. It is imperative that any report card designations do not discriminate.
- Teachers *must* explain modified grades to parents.
- You may put info on reports that go home, but not on the permanent record.

Examples:
- Give a kid a calculator = NO impact on the grades
- Oral vs. written = NO impact on grades
- Reducing # of problems = NO impact on grades
- Consistently and significantly reduce the number of vocabulary words learned in English = May impact grades
- If the kid is meeting 2/3 of the curriculum, let it go.

Grading systems for all students must have a rationale that addresses both standards and special needs and be implemented throughout a school.

Research indicates that grading policies and practices, including adaptations, should be clearly explained to all students before they are made, with a compelling rationale provided. Because both teachers and students seem to feel that effort should be recognized in some way, this may be a good place to start for reaching some consensus about grading adaptations.

Same subject,
Same curriculum,
Same level: Different teacher

Will all students be graded the same? Equally?

What's fair?

---

[1] Adapted from *Successful Co-Teaching Strategies* by Dr. Marilyn Friend, < www.marilynfriend.com>.

WHAT IS FAIR?

In studies done by Munk, Bursuck, and Olson, the following observations were made: [2]
Teachers may change grading criteria by

- Varying grading weights (e.g., varying how much certain criteria count toward a grade).
- Modifying curricular expectations (e.g., identifying an individualized curriculum on which to base a grade).
- Using contracts and modified course syllabi (e.g., teacher and student agreeing on quality, quantity, and timelines for specific work).
- Grading based on improvement (e.g., assigning extra points for improvement over previous performance).

In addition to changes made to the criteria for grading, teachers may adapt the actual letter and number grades by

- Adding written comments (e.g., adding comments to clarify the criteria used to determine a letter grade).
- Adding information from a student activity log (e.g., keeping written anecdotal notes indicating student performance in specific areas over time).
- Adding information from portfolios or performance-based assessments (e.g., collecting student work that measures effort and progress).
- Under some circumstances, teachers may elect to implement alternatives to letter and number grades. Such adaptations include pass-fail grades and competency checklists.

Teachers felt the following adaptations were most helpful to students with disabilities:
- Pass-fail grades
- Checklists
- Written comments

Teachers indicated that letter and number grades could be adapted for students with disabilities (in descending order of perceived helpfulness) by
- Basing grade on process versus product.
- Basing grade on amount of improvement.
- Basing grade on progress on Individualized Education Program (I.E.P.) objectives.
- Adjusting grading weights based on assignment and ability.
- Basing grade on criteria defined in an individual contract.

---

[2] DENNIS D. MUNK AND WILLIAM D. BURSUCK, "Report Card Grading Adaptations for Students with Disabilities: Types and Acceptability", Intervention in School & Clinic, 1 May 1998.

Adapted from WILLIAM D. BURSUCK, DENNIS D. MUNK, AND MARY M. OLSON, "The Fairness of Report Card Grading Adaptations: What Do Students With and Without Learning Disabilities Think?" Remedial & Special Education, 1 Mar 1999.

Note: The demographics of this study include one high school of 2000+ students and therefore may not be reflective of the general population.

Teachers indicated that letter and number/percentage grades are more useful for students without disabilities, whereas pass/fail grades are more useful for students with disabilities.

Regarding fairness, 73% of the teachers felt that making report card adaptations *only* for students with disabilities was unfair. Most teachers however said that the reason that the adaptations would be unfair was that adaptations were made available only to students with disabilities, not necessarily, because they represented a lowering of standards or a lack of consistency. *In fact, 50% of the teachers reported using specific adaptations for students without disabilities.* ***This finding suggests that teachers may be quite flexible when they think adaptations will benefit [all] their students.***

Consider this:

If a teacher ***adapts*** by using knowledge and guiding principles of learning style, multiple intelligences, and brain-based research, couldn't that teacher consistently ***adapt*** for all students as their needs indicate? Would that not be fair?

Assessment Accommodations

WHAT IS AN ASSESSMENT ACCOMMODATION?

- An assessment accommodation is an alteration in the way a test is administered or the way a student takes a test.
- Assessment accommodations are designed to respond to a student need. Assessment accommodations generally refer to changes that do not alter what the test measures.
- They are not intended to give the student an unfair advantage.
- Students with disabilities may use assessment accommodations to show what they know without being impeded by their disabilities
- I.E.P.'s must include a statement of any individual modifications in the administration of state or district-wide assessments of student achievement that are needed in order for the child to participate in the assessment.
- In general, no accommodation should ever be recommended for a student unless that student also has an opportunity to use it during instructional activities.

GUIDING PRINCIPLES

- Do not assume that every student with disabilities needs assessment accommodations.
- The I.E.P. team must determine the accommodations.
- Base accommodations on student need.
- Be respectful of the student's cultural and ethnic background.
- Integrate assessment accommodations into classroom instruction.
- Know whether your state and/or district has an approved list of accommodations.
- Plan early for accommodations.
- Include students in decision-making.
- Understand the purpose of the assessment.

- Request only those accommodations that are truly needed.
- Determine if the selected accommodation requires another accommodation.
- Provide practice opportunities for the student.
- Remember that accommodations in test taking won't necessarily eliminate frustration for the student.

Educate students about the purpose of accommodations. Assure them that the accommodations aren't just for "stupid" kids. If they need privacy to use an accommodation, try to change the setting so that perceived stigma is reduced. ***Consider if teachers make accommodations on a regular basis in their classrooms based on students' learning styles and multiple intelligences, then there will be much less stigma attached to the student who chooses to use a needed accommodation.***

- Student input is critical in selecting accommodations. If a student does not like an accommodation, he or she will not use it.
- Two key questions to ask a student about a proposed accommodation are:
  - "Does this help you?"
  - "Will you use this accommodation?"

TYPES OF ACCOMMODATIONS

Timing accommodations
- Frequent breaks
- Extended time

Scheduling accommodations
- Over Several Days
- Order of Subtests
- Specific Time of Day

Setting accommodations
- Preferential Seating
- Separate location
- Specialized Setting

Presentation accommodations
- Different editions
- Read test/directions

Presentation accommodations (Cont.)
- Prompts
- Clarification
- Templates
- Markers
- Secure Paper to Desk
- Magnifying/amplification devices
- Reread directions

Response accommodations
- Student marks booklet
- Verbal response
- Special paper
- Math tools
- Reference materials
- Technology
- Point to answer

Most states have an approved list of accommodations.
These can vary widely from one state to the next.

Specific Test Adaptations

- One-on-one oral testing.
- Add a word bank.
- Highlight multiple-choice items.
- Peer "test" using a game such as "3-card match".
- Break the test into smaller chunks.
- Add white space.
- Make sure directions and phrasing is clear and concrete.
- Read the test orally to a small group.
- Assign a project that demonstrates learning.
- Create crossword format tests and quizzes.
- Provide pictures as cues.
- Weighed grading of tests: only grade what student is accountable for and/or for concepts tested rather than quantity of test items.
- Use portfolio assessment.
- Use performance assessments.
- Allow the use of spell checker or word processor for essay questions.
- Give individual help with directions during tests.
- Read test questions to students.
- Simplify wording of test questions.
- Give practice questions as a study guide.
- Give extra help preparing for tests.
- Provide extended time to finish tests.
- Use black-and-white copies.
- Give feedback to individual student during test.
- Highlight key words in questions.
- Allow use of learning aids during tests (e.g., calculators, word processors).
- Give frequent quizzes rather than relying on exams.
- Allow students to answer fewer questions while still covering all content.
- Allow oral instead of written answers (e.g., tape recorders).
- Give the actual test as a study guide.
- Change the question type (e.g., essay to multiple choice or multiple choice to essay) with the opportunity to answer orally.
- Teach students test-taking skills.
- Use tests with enlarged print.
- Test on lesser content than rest of the class.
- Provide extra space on tests for answering.
- Give open-book/notes tests.
- Allow answers in outline format.
- Give take-home tests.

Note. Adapted from Jayanthi et al. (in press).

Grading Options Quick List

- Give a separate grade for process and for product/content
  - A math test has one grade for "demonstrated work" and another grade for final answers.
  - An English paper has one grade based on the steps the student completed to fulfill the rubric or paper's requirements and another grade for the final product.
  - A science lab may have one grade to reflect the attention to detail, effort, patience and neatness of the lab and another grade for the final product.
  - *Teachers typically grade only the final product. Grading for both motivates and gives credit to students for their efforts on the assignment or test.
- Grade on improvement shown.
- Grade on effort shown.
- Traditional letter grading system
- Pass/Fail options
- Differentiated Syllabi – Contract for grades based on syllabi chosen. Content Same –Process Different
- Weighted grades within the class setting – ex: Major tests count least; class work counts most.
- Co-teachers share grading.
- Portfolio summaries
- Grade based on rubrics.
- Grades adjusted to student ability
- Grades are based on less content than the rest of the class.
- Grade based on I.E.P. goals.
- Give audio feedback on drafts of tests and projects before final grading.
- Use the MEDIAN instead of the MEAN for grading.

Which grade truly reflects the student's overall knowledge?

78	98	100
78	93	93
75	88	80
75	86	80
73	62	80
72	0	79
69	Median 87	75
68	Mean: 71	63
45		60
0		0
Median: 72.5		0
Mean: 63		Median: 79
		Mean: 65

TEST TAKING FIRST AID KIT

1 pack of Smarties Candies - to boost your test taking brain power
1 pencil -- to help you record the knowledge you have learned
1 sticker -- to help you stick with the task at hand
1 eraser -- to use when you check over your work
1 Hershey's Hug -- for all the hard work you put into the test
1 highlighter -- to highlight all your success
1 pencil grip -- to get a grip on the task at hand

FOR BEST RESULTS, COMBINE WITH:

1 night of restful sleep
1 nutritious breakfast
1 positive attitude

POSSIBLE SIDE EFFECTS:
Improved Test-taking Skills, Good Grades

AN ALTERNATIVE TO THE TRADITIONAL QUIZ

The best alternative to testing is demonstration of knowledge. Whenever possible, have students do a project, write a paper, do an analysis, apply knowledge learned. Here's a fun and effective way to quiz students.

THREE CARD MATCH: PEER TUTOR OR PEER QUIZ

Materials:
- Matching cards
- Quarter (coin)

Instructions
- Pair up students. (Matching ability is not necessary and may be less successful.)
- Allow students to peer practice by matching the cards before the "quiz".
- Students MUST insure each one of their pair knows how to match all the cards.
- Instruct students that once a pair of students is confident that they can match the cards each on their own, they should notify you that they are ready for the quiz.
- Have the pair call heads or tails.
- Flip a coin.
- The person who calls tails takes the quiz.
- That student has to match the cards by himself/herself on the spot for you to see.
- Both students get the same quiz grade.

Culture and Language Bias as Barriers To Learning

According to a study reported by Barbara Keough of UCLA, teaching young children testing skills totally devoid of content can lead to substantial score increases. Working with a group of Hispanic children, she reported, "We trained one group of youngsters in testing experiences. The training was totally non-content. We got a whopping main effect. When the children who had been trained to take tests were tested they did extraordinarily well...Such findings raise issues regarding what's being assessed, and how much of early screening is really testing a child's aptitude and how much is an indication of school experiences related to taking tests" (Communique, Dec. 1988).[3]

Other questions to consider:
- Are you testing learned social studies content, or reading ability?
- Are you testing understanding of the math process or the ability to memorize formulas?
- Are you testing a student's writing ability or her understanding of the novel the class read?

---

[3] <http://www.fairtest.org/examarts/winter89/K-12.html>.

A concerned teacher writes

I student taught 3rd grade in a very low socioeconomic elementary school. We used a testing support curriculum titled Target Teach. For 5 weeks, we would teach the objectives. The 6th week we would test, called a benchmark, on those specific objectives. During the second six weeks, we talked about proper and common nouns and the appropriate capitalization. So of course the students learned that islands was a common noun because it did not name a specific island, city was a common noun because it does not name a specific city, and state was a common noun because it did not name a specific state. On the second benchmark test, the following question appeared:

Where is the error in capitalization?
a) My friends and I
b) Traveled to the Virgin Islands
c) For vacation.
d) No mistakes

Of course, my students marked (d) as the correct answer. They had never had any experience at all with the Virgin Islands. Most of them had never been to the other side of our city! Even the top reader in my class, who was reading on a 4th grade level, did not answer this question correctly.

I have another example, but it's not one that I witnessed myself. I have a teaching friend in SC who shared this with me when I was telling her about my experience. She works with VERY poor young students, either kindergarten or 1st grade, in the foothills. On their standardized test, there was a picture of a refrigerator, a cap, a horse, and a television. Since these students were pre-readers, she was administering the test orally. She told them to fill in the circle of the picture of the refrigerator. Well, these children are not familiar with that term. They call it an icebox. Of course, they had no idea what a refrigerator was, so they just answered anything.
Natalie

Bias is the presence of some characteristic of an item on a test or assignment that results in differential performance for individuals of the same ability but from different ethnic, sex, cultural, or religious groups.

Bias comes in many forms. It can be sex, cultural, ethnic, religious, or class bias. An item may be biased if it contains content or language that is for certain groups of students but not others. It might also be biased if the item structure or format is more difficult for subgroups of students being tested. An example of content bias against girls would be one in which students are asked to compare the weights of several objects, including a football. Since girls are less likely to have handled a football, they might find the item more difficult than boys, even though they have mastered the concept measured by the item (Scheuneman, 1982a)[4].

Stereotypes found in test or classroom materials might offend or turn off students to the learning and assessment the teacher is trying to achieve. Classroom materials and tests should be free of material that may be offensive, demeaning, or emotionally charged.

---

[4] Scheuneman, J.D. (1982a). A new look at bias in aptitude tests. In P. Merrifield (Ed.), "New directions for testing and measurement: Measuring human abilities," No. 12. San Francisco: Jossey-Bass.

When developing tests and handouts, or reviewing ready made materials ask yourself the following questions to guide you in using unbiased material.[5]

- Do any of the questions contain content that is different or unfamiliar to any students in the classroom?
- Will students of varying backgrounds get the item correct or incorrect for the wrong reason?
- Does the content of the question, material, or instructions contain information and/or skills that may not be expected to be within all the students' backgrounds?
- Does the assignment or test contain words that have different or unfamiliar meanings for any of my student population?
- Do test questions have difficult vocabulary that is not intended to be tested? Sometimes students get items on a test incorrect not because they did not know the answer, but rather, because they did not understand the question.
- Is the question free of culturally exclusive or specific language, vocabulary, or reference pronouns?
- Are the test instructions clear or phrased in a way that they will be understood by all the student population?

The section on bias is based on Hambleton, R.K. and Rogers, H.J. (1996) "Developing an Item Bias Review Form," which is available through ERIC/AE.

I highly recommend the The National Center for Fair & Open Testing as a source of information on State Assessment and standardized testing. <http://www.fairtest.org/index.htm>

The National Center for Fair & Open Testing (FairTest) is an advocacy organization working to end the abuses, misuses, and flaws of standardized testing and ensure that evaluation of students and workers is fair, open, and educationally sound.

FairTest places special emphasis on eliminating the racial, class, gender, and cultural barriers to equal opportunity posed by standardized tests and preventing their damage to the quality of education. Based on four Goals and Principles, they provide information, technical assistance, and advocacy on a broad range of testing concerns focusing on three areas: K-12, university admissions, and employment tests, including teacher testing.

---

[5] Adapted from " Item Bias Review" by Hambleton, Ronald - Rodgers, Jane, 1995-10-00: ED398241:ERIC Clearinghouse on Assessment and Evaluation Washington DC.

APPENDIX-- Famous People

1. _____

2. _____

3. _____

4. _____

5. _____

6. _____

7. _____

8. _____

9. _____

To download the complete activity go to www.aimhieducational.com/inclusion.html

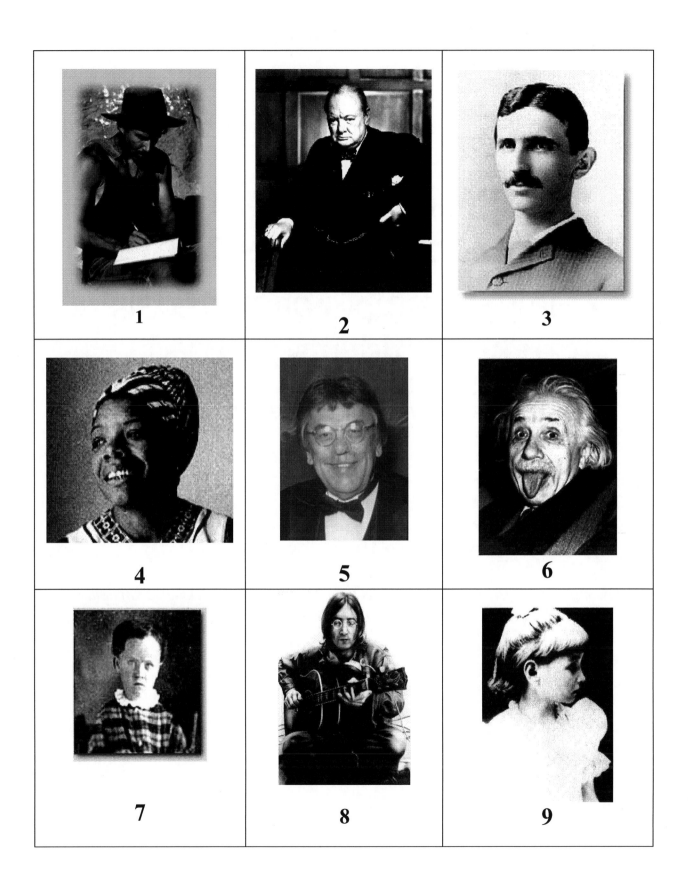

1

2

3

4

5

6

7

8

9

TIP TO MAINTAIN ATTENTION WHILE REVIEWING INSTRUCTIONS

Put Prompts on Materials (or teach students to do it)

- Simple prompts on materials can help students succeed.

 Star at the starting point.

Arrow to indicate direction.

START HERE ✓ Green mark to keep going

- Bullets

These prompts are presented in different colors. Simply the act of picking up different color highlighters or markers works to keep students involved and attentive.

Multiple Intelligences

Linguistic:
- Tells tall tales, jokes and stories
- Has a good memory
- Enjoys word games
- Enjoys reading and writing
- Has a good vocabulary for his/her age
- Has good verbal communication
- Enjoys crossword puzzles
- Appreciates nonsense rhymes, puns, tongue twisters, etc.
- Spells words accurately (or if preschool, spells using sounds that is advanced for age)

Logical-Mathematical:
- Asks questions about how things work
- Enjoys math activities
- Enjoys playing chess, checkers, or other strategy games
- Enjoys logic puzzles or brain teasers
- Uses higher-order thinking skills
- Interested in patterns, categories and relationships
- Likes doing and creating experiments
- Does arithmetic problems in his or her head quickly (or if preschool, math concepts are advanced for age)
- Has a good sense of cause and effect

Bodily Kinesthetic:
- Excels in one or more sports or physical arts
- Moves, twitches, taps or fidgets while seated for a long time
- Enjoys taking things apart and putting them back together
- Touches new objects
- Enjoys running, jumping or wrestling
- Expresses him or herself dramatically
- Enjoys modeling clay and finger painting
- Good with his or her hands
- Cleverly mimics other people's gestures or mannerisms
- Reports different physical sensations while thinking or working

Spatial:
- Daydreams more than peers
- Enjoys art activities, puzzles and mazes
- Likes visual presentations
- Understands more from pictures than words while reading
- Doodles on paper
- Loves construction sets: Legos, K'nex, Capsela, etc.
- Often inventing things
- Draws things that are advanced for age
- Reads maps, charts, and diagrams more easily than text (or if preschool, enjoys looking at more than text)

Musical:
- Recognizes off-key music
- Remembers melodies
- Plays a musical instrument or sings in a choir.
- Speaks or moves rhythmically
- Taps rhythmically as he or she works
- Is sensitive to environmental noise
- Responds favorably to music
- Sings songs that he or she has learned outside of the classroom
- Is a discriminating listener
- Creates his or her own songs and melodies

Interpersonal:
- Enjoys socializing with peers
- Acts as a natural leader
- Gives advice to friends who have problems
- Seems to be street-smart
- Belongs to clubs, committees, or other organizations
- Likes to play games with other kids
- Has one or more close friends
- Shows concern for others
- Perceives and makes distinctions in people's moods, intentions and motivations
- Good at responding to other people's feelings

Intrapersonal:
- Displays a sense of independence or a strong will
- Has a realistic sense of his or her strengths
- Has a good sense of self-direction
- Prefers working alone to working with others, may be shy
- Learns from his failures and successes
- Is insightful and self-aware
- Adapts well to his or her environment
- Aware of own emotions, strengths, and limitations
- Is self-disciplined
- Marches to the beat of different drummer in his/her style of living and learning

Naturalist:
- Enjoys labeling and identifying nature
- Sensitive to changes in weather
- Good at distinguishing among cars, sneakers, and jewelry, etc.

Existentialist (possible 9th intelligence) –
- Learns in the context of where humankind stands in the "big picture" of existence. Asks "Why are we here?" and "What is our role in the world?"
- This intelligence is seen in the discipline of philosophy.

DIFFERENTIATING FOR MULTIPLE INTELLIGENCES

Suggestions for Assignments (Based on Multiple Intelligences)

For Verbal/Linguistic Learners
- Allow options for students to choose from when assigning projects, research, study, and practice.
- Create Radio or TV advertisements (See History Project below).
- Debate current events.
- Create crossword puzzles.
- Teach the class the steps to….
- Write a script.

For Logical Mathematical Learners
- Compare and contrast ideas.
- Create a time line.
- Classify concepts/objects/materials.
- Read or design maps.
- Create a computer program.
- Create story problems for….
- Design and conduct an experiment on…..
- Use a Venn diagram to explain….
- Teach using technology.

For Body Kinesthetic Learners
- Create hands on projects.
- Conduct hands on experiments.
- Create human sculptures to illustrate situations.
- Design something that requires applying math concepts.
- Re-enact great moments from history.
- Study body language from different cultural situations.
- Make task or puzzle cards for….

For Visual Spatial Learners
- Make visual organizer or memory model of the material being learned. (Give copies to other students in the class).
- Graph the results of a survey or results from a course of study.
- Create posters or flyers.
- Create collages.
- Draw maps.
- Study the art of a culture.
- Color-code the process of….

For Musical Rhythmic Learners
- Create "raps" (key dates, math, poems).
- Identify social issues through lyrics.
- Analyze different historical periods through their music.
- Make up sounds for different math operations or processes.
- Use music to enhance the learning of….
- Write a new ending to a song so that it explains….

For Interpersonal Learners
- Analyze a story.
- Review a material/concepts/books orally.
- Discuss/debate controversial issues.
- Find relationships between objects, cultures, situations.
- Role-play a conversation with an important historical figure.
- Solve complex word problems in a group.
- Peer Tutor the subject being learned.

For Intrapersonal Learners
- Keep a journal to demonstrate learning.
- Analyze historical personalities.
- Imagine self as character in history, or scientist discovering a cure, or mathematician working a theory and describe or write about what you imagine to demonstrate learning.

For Naturalist Learners
- Sort and classify content in relation to the natural world.
- Interact with nature through field trips.
- Encourage learning in natural surroundings.
- Categorize facts about….

METHODS FOR TEACHING INTROVERTS AND EXTROVERTS

Inter and Intra personal learners, Verbal Linguistic, and that incorporate Brain based research, and fosters long term retention of course content

TAPPS

- Teacher poses question and provides quiet time for students.
- Teacher designates the explainer and listener within each pair.
- Explainers explain ideas to listeners. Listeners can (1) ask questions of clarification, (2) disagree, or (3) provide hints when explainers become lost.
- Teacher critiques some explainers' answers and provides closure.

NOMINAL GROUP METHOD

- Teachers pose questions and provide quiet time for students.
- Each team member shares ideas with others in a round-robin fashion.
- Teams discuss ideas and reach closure.
- Teacher critiques some teams' answers and provides closure.

THINK PAIR SHARE

Think/Pair/Share is a strategy designed to provide students with "food for thought" on a given topic. This enables students to formulate their own ideas and share them with another student.

- Teacher poses a question to the class/group.
- Teacher gives students 1-2 minutes to think about the questions and make some personal connections.
- Teacher instructs the students to form pairs and share their thinking with each other.
OPTIONS:
- Students form new pairs and share again.
- After think pair share, class as a whole joins in discussion.

For more Think/Pair/Share ideas go to http://home.att.net/~clnetwork/thinkps.htm

JIG SAW

Jigsaw is a cooperative learning strategy that incorporates the most effective method of learning according to brain-based research: *I learn when I teach it.* Students meet with members of other groups who are assigned the same topic, and after mastering the material, return to the original group and teach the material to the original group members.

- Divide students into groups of four.
- Assign a topic or section of material to each group member.
- Each student finds other students with the same topic or section and forms a new group of "experts".
- This new group learns together, becoming experts on their topic.
- Once students are comfortable with the material, they rejoin their original group.
- Student topic experts teach their original group the subject matter.

**Several short jig saw events with manageable chunks of subject matter might be more effective than assigning large amounts of material.

OPTION
- Students in a group are each given a different paragraph from a reading selection, or different paragraphs offering different views of the same subject.
- Students read their paragraph silently.
- Students then explain what they read to the rest of the group.
(This option requires confident readers.)

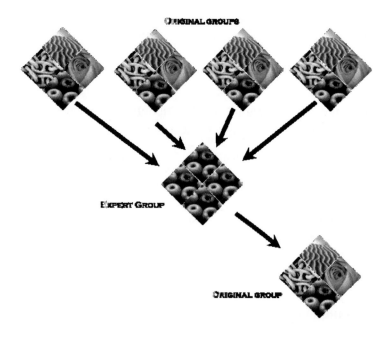

ORIGINAL GROUPS

EXPERT GROUP

ORIGINAL GROUP

PEER PRACTICE ACTIVITY

PEER PRACTICE IN ASTRONOMY

TASK B QUESTIONS	TASK A ANSWERS
UNIVERSE	A hot, glowing globe of gas that emits energy
SUPERCLUSTER	The sun and its collection of 9 planets
LOCAL GROUP	An object that revolves around a star
GALAXY (Milky Way)	Study of everything beyond the earth
SUN'S NEIGHBORS	Groupings of stars based upon the imagination of man

PEER PRACTICE IN ASTRONOMY

TASK A QUESTIONS	TASK B ANSWERS
STAR (Sun)	All of space and what is found in it
SOLAR SYSTEM	A collection of galaxies, which include the local group
PLANET (Earth)	The Milky Way and its twenty closest neighbors
ASTRONOMY	A vast collection of stars, gas, and dust
CONSTELLATION	The sun and its twenty closest neighbors

Instructions

- Create practice sheets as above with the QUESTIONS (in short hand) on one side and answers to those QUESTIONS on the other side of the PARTNER sheet and visa versa.
- Have students fold the sheets down the middle so that they are looking at only questions or answers.
- For example, one partner looks at TASK A questions and the other partner looks at TASK B answers.
- Students quiz each other by mixing up the order they ask the questions or cue with the answers.
- Keep QUESTIONS and answers to 5-7 chunks of information on one sheet.

**Save yourself some work: Have students create their own practice sheets then photocopy for the class.

TEACHING EACH OTHER...

- Students are pre-arranged in pairs.
- Assign partner A and partner B.
- Teach 10 minutes – Stop.
- Set Timer for 1-2 minutes.
- Partner A teach Partner B one thing that you've taught them in the past 10 min.
- Set timer for 1-2 minutes.
- Class shares what they learned.
- Repeat for one more round.

METHODS FOR TEACHING SENSING TYPES

Visual Spatial Learners, and incorporates Brain based research

WHAT MUST BE KNOWN (WMBK) METHOD

1. Ask: What is (are) the topic's most essential general principle(s) or goals?
2. Place the answer in a goal box.
3. Ask: What topic(s) do the students need to know in order to achieve the goal?
4. Place these subgoal boxes below the goal box and show an arrow leading from each subgoal box to the goal box.
5. Continue to ask WMBK questions until you connect with material previously covered. Present new subject material by starting at the bottom of the diagram and work up towards the goal box.

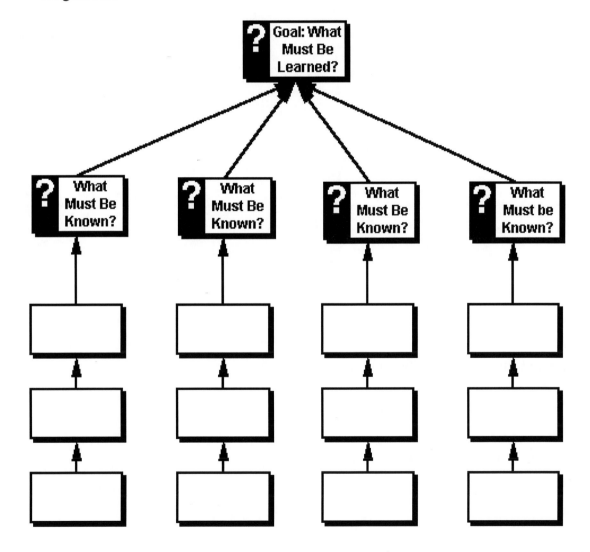

KWHL METHOD

K	W	H	L
What I Know	**What I Want to** **find out** **or** **What I Want to Solve**	**How will I find information?** (Which resources, web pages, texts, formulas, methods, etc.) If reading, how can you find out what we want to learn?	**What I Learned**

What is the question or problem that you are trying to answer or solve?
What attributes or characteristics do you expect to use?

(NOTE: Make sure that everything you write above will help you answer this question.)

THE APPLICATION-THEORY-APPLICATION A-T-A METHOD

1. Present a problem or mini-case (Application) to the class.
2. Students attempt to analyze and solve the case or problem **without** the benefit of the upcoming chapter's theory or ideas.
3. The problem or mini-case *motivates* sensing students to learn the material.
4. Applications answer the question that sensing students often ask, "Why am I learning this material?"
5. After the class has struggled with the problem (and sometimes emerged victoriously), present the chapter's (T)heory or ideas, and then apply it to the original application.
6. Afterwards, present additional (A)pplications and have the students apply the theory.

An opening application problem or mini-case should (1) be familiar to students, (2) engage their curiosity, (3) be **almost** solvable from previous text material or student experiences, and (4) be baffling, or counter-intuitive, if possible. A familiar problem assures sensing students that their experiences have prepared them to address the problem. Being "almost solvable" minimizes students' frustrations. The application should be "just beyond a student's reach". However, previously learned material or experiences should help students make a reasonable solution attempt. An application that is too significant a leap will cause frustration and the feeling that the teacher is playing games with the students.

ADVANCED ORGANIZERS AS DEFINED BY DAVID AUSUBEL

- The most general ideas of a subject should be presented first and then progressively differentiated in terms of detail and specifics.
- Instructional materials should attempt to integrate new material with previously presented information through comparisons and cross-referencing of new and old ideas.

Develop advance organizers by answering the following questions:
1. What do students know that at a very general level is similar to the subject matter about to be taught?
2. How can I demonstrate the connections between what is known and what is to be learned?

PROVIDE A SYLLABUS

Use Videos to Provide Background Information

Break into chunks with due dates

NAME_____World History/Textbook Assignments

Follow each set of directions below for work in the textbook. Also, pay attention to the due dates as listed. These will be graded assignments. Many are "thought" questions, so be careful to read and answer what is being asked.

Due Friday, May 5, 2000
> Chapter 21
> Use the chapter to help you do the following assignments on pages 686-687.
>> ☐ Using Key Terms: Do # 1-17
>> ☐ Reviewing the facts: Do # 5, 7, and 8

Due Monday, May 8, 2000
> Chapter 22
>> ☐ Read page 688
>> ☐ Read page 691   ☐ Answer question #3
>> ☐ Read page 694   ☐ Answer question #2
>> ☐ Read page 702-703   ☐ Answer question #4
>> ☐ Read page 704-705   ☐ Answer question #3
>> ☐ Read page 706-707   ☐ Answer question #2
>> ☐ Read page 719-720

Due Tuesday, May 9, 2000
> Chapter 22, continued
> Use the chapter to help you do the following assignments on pages 726-727
>> ☐ Reviewing the Facts: do #'s 2, 5, 7, 9, 13
>> ☐ Thinking critically: do #'s 1, 9

Due Wednesday, May 10, 2000
> Use chapters 23 and 24 to gain a definition and understanding of the following terms: COLONIALISM and IMPERIALISM
> Write notes down to explain each one.

COLONIALISM	IMPERIALISM

Contributed by Barbara Mee, Social Studies Teacher, Londonderry High School

---

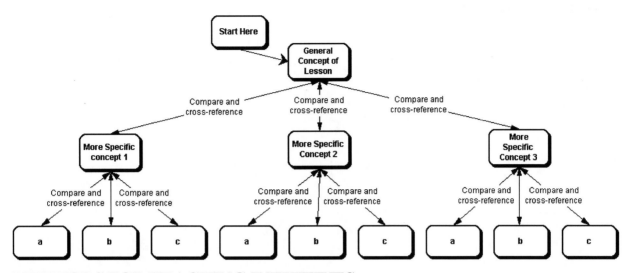

METHODS FOR TEACHING INTUITIVES:

Interpersonal learners and that incorporate Brain based research, and fosters long term retention of course content, logical mathematical, Verbal Linguistic. Use the mind maps and add Visual Spatial

THE SMALL GROUP DISCOVER METHOD

Neil Davidson developed the small group discovery method in 1967 at the University of Wisconsin. He started with the idea established by R.L. Moore that bright students can develop mathematics. He then changed the social environment to render the idea workable for much larger numbers of students in undergraduate courses.

The discovery method concept can be successful for math problems, science case studies, social studies "investigations" or mysteries, and alternative solutions for conflicts in literature.

- Divide the class into small groups of 3-4.
- Each group discusses the problem to be solved (theorem) and proves it cooperatively as a group effort during class.
- Every group has its own section of the black board for working space.
- Members write a group solution on the board for each problem.
- Teacher moves from group to group checking solutions (proofs) on the board and gives suggestions for improvement, ask probing questions to help guide, or give hints.
- Design problems that can be solved in one class period.

Advantage: A group of students will solve a problem that each of the group members would give up on if he or she was working on it by himself or herself.

OVERVIEW METHOD

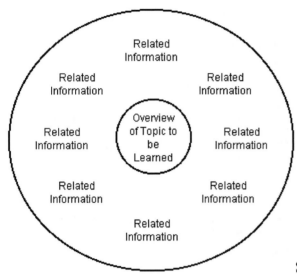

Start with an overview of the topic.

METHODS FOR TEACHING THINKING TYPES

- Define clear objectives. Using Bloom's Taxonomy will help with this.
- Have action-oriented lessons.
- List pros and cons as related to your topic.
- Don't ramble or go off on tangents. It drives thinking types crazy or you lose them.
- Structure class material logically.

METHODS FOR TEACHING FEELING TYPES

- Provide opportunity for interaction. (See methods for Introverts and Extraverts.)
- Place importance on class harmony. (See chapter "Social Considerations.")
- Be friendly and collaborative.
- Show the impact of whatever you are teaching on people, especially why it is important to the individuals involved.
- Express appreciation for student contributions.

METHODS FOR TEACHING JUDGING TYPES

Also incorporates fundamentals of Brain based research

SPEED WRITING

Most students can learn speedwriting in several minutes. Just omit all (or most) vowels. Or develop your own shorthand method. For example, <u>mst stdnts cn lrn spdwrtng in svrl mnts. Jst omt ll or mst vwls.</u>

SPLIT PAGE

Draw a line down center of a notebook page. On the left-hand side, record the lecture (use speedwriting or your own shorthand notation). After class, write a **commentary** on the right-hand side. Include restating ideas in your own words, finding sources of confusion, identifying key points, looking for links to earlier learned material, and asking what does this mean to me (the student).

COLOR CODING

Use different colors to record ideas presented in class and found in the text or readings. For example, use blue to code major ideas and green to code links to previously learned material.

AOR MODEL

In answering an essay question, first **A**nalyze the question and jot down key ideas, **O**rganize the ideas into a logical sequence, and only then write the essay (**R**espond).

REVERSE QUESTION

To review an essay question, first read your answer. Then construct an essay question based on your answer. Now compare your question to the teacher's question. If different, revise your answer. This strategy ensures that students answer the teacher's question.

TREATING OBJECTIVE QUESTIONS AS ESSAY QUESTION

Read the question's stem (the portion that contains the question) and write a brief answer. Then compare your answer to the four or five choices, and select the answer most similar to your mini-essay.

METHODS FOR TEACHING PERCEPTIVES

- Break down assignments.
- Help students set goals.
- Teach them to use organizers.
- Use audio tapes to give frequent feedback.

USE AUDIO CASSETTE TAPES FOR FEEDBACK ON ASSIGNMENTS.

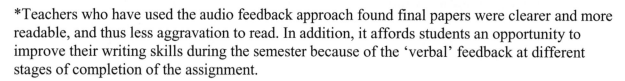

- Students hand-in an audiotape with their sub-assignments.
- While reading the assignment, make comments on the audiotape (We speak faster than we can write) on content and grammar.

*Teachers who have used the audio feedback approach found final papers were clearer and more readable, and thus less aggravation to read. In addition, it affords students an opportunity to improve their writing skills during the semester because of the 'verbal' feedback at different stages of completion of the assignment.

GENERAL TYPE CONSIDERATIONS FOR TEACHERS

- Extraverts need dialogue.
- Introverts need time to think.
- Intuitives are way ahead of you.
- Sensing types and judging types need a sense of structure in the instruction; uncertainty about organization of lesson will discourage learning.
- Feeling types need human contact; failure to communicate on a personal level will discourage learning.
- Thinking types need answers to questions that make sense; learning is business, not personal.
- Stop at frequent intervals and ask for questions. Asking students by name for questions will help to involve the introverts.
- Make frequent reference to a lesson outline. Point out when digression from outline begins and when it ends.
- Point out, as questions are asked in class, how it has helped in contributing to the lesson. This makes feeling types feel very valuable.
- Use the reflection method to rephrase questions. This will help clarify for sensing types what is being asked.
- Develop collaborative learning exercises that require the use of concepts taught.

Information about Personality Preference and Learning style was adapted from *The Master Teacher*, by Harvey J. Brightman, Georgia State University, and *Implications of Personality Type for Teaching and Learning* by John W. Pelley, Ph.D., Texas Tech University Health Sciences Center, and the Myers-Briggs Type Indicator description pamphlets.

Tools & Techniques that Help Students Focus

BRAIN GYM®

BRAIN GYMNASTICS : A Wakeup Call to the Brain[1]

Brain Gym® is a series of exercises that enables the brain to work at its best. The techniques are a composite of many differing sciences based predominantly upon neurobiology. It has been found to facilitate learning in learning-disabled children. However, the results of using Brain Gym(R) have proven to be highly effective for all learners. There is even evidence that Brain Gym(R) can be used for psychological disorders as well.

Teachers will find these exercises enhance student performance before test taking in particular, but also they work before listening to lectures and studying. It also may relieve stress.

How does it work? Carla Hannaford, Ph.D., neurophysiologist, states in "Smart Moves." that our bodies are very much a part of all our learning, and learning is not an isolated "brain" function. Every nerve and cell is a network contributing to our intelligence and our learning capability. She states, "movement activates the neural wiring throughout the body, making the whole body the instrument of learning". Carla states that "sensation" forms the basis of concepts from which "thinking" evolves.

Brain Gym® exercises consider our bi-cameral brain. The brain has a left and a right hemisphere, each one doing certain distinct tasks. Often one side of our brain works more than the other depending upon the tasks we are doing or on how we have developed as human beings. If the two brains are working fully and sharing information across the Corpus Collosum, then there is a balance of brain function. Without this balance, there is always going to be something that is not understood or remembered. Brain Gym® assists in integrating the two brains which gives us full capacity for problem solving or learning.

We are also "electrical" beings and our brain's neurons work by electrical connections. Water has been found to be the best thing we can do to facilitate the thinking process because of its capacity to conduct electricity and assist cell function. As Carla Hannaford says, "Water comprises more of the brain (with estimates of 90%) than of any other organ of the body." Thus, a simple drink

---

[1] Adapted from an article by Ruth Trimble (trimble@hawaii.edu).

Much of the factual material for this article is taken from "Smart Moves" by Carla Hannaford, Ph.D. and Dr. Paul Dennison and his EduK(R) literature. Please cite these authors when using this material. In Honolulu there are several very good Brain Gym(R) instructors and their addresses & numbers will be listed at the end of this document. Permission to use my data is given, but it constitutes only my opinion and limited practical experience and is not in any way intended to represent the official Brain Gym(R) or EduK(R) view nor give permission to reproduce the detailed exercises designed by the other authors without citing them.

---

of water before a test or before going to class can have a profound effect on our brain's readiness to work. Unfortunately, coffee or soda will have the opposite effect since these will upset the electrolytes in the brain. In all, then the exercises that you see here are designed to make us whole-brain learners. Some simple but effective ways to wake-up the brain and get it all working at once and optimally:

Before any of the following exercises, DRINK a glass of water.

"BRAIN BUTTONS"

This exercise helps the Carotid arteries to open and function better in sending blood to the brain, and it also helps lower blood pressure.

1. Put one hand so that there is as wide a space as possible between the thumb and index finger.
2. Then place your index and thumb into the slight indentations below the collarbone on each side of the sternum.
3. Press lightly in a pulsing manner.
4. At the same time put the other hand over the navel area of the stomach.
5. Gently press on these points for about 2 minutes.

"HOOK-UPS"

This works well for nerves before a test or special event such as making a speech. Anytime there is nervousness or anxiety, this will calm.

1. Sit for this activity and cross the right leg over the left at the ankles.
2. Take your right wrist and cross it over the left wrist and link up the fingers so that the right wrist is on top.
3. Now bend the elbows out and gently turn the fingers in towards the body until they rest on the sternum (breast bone) in the center of the chest.
4. Stay in this position.
5. Touch your tongue to your palate.
6. Breathe in through your nose and out through your mouth in slow, deep, belly breaths.
7. Keep the ankles crossed and the wrists crossed and then breathe evenly in this position for a few minutes.
8. You will be noticeably calmer after that time.

"CROSS CRAWL"

This exercise assists the Corpus Callosum [the muscle that connects the two brains,] by forcing signals to pass between the brains and cross over the mid-point.

1. You can stand or sit for this. Put the right hand across the body to the left knee as you raise it, and then do the same thing for the left hand on the right knee just as if you were marching.
2. Just do this either sitting or standing for about 2 minutes.

Ruth Trimble states, "My student test scores have gone up because of Brain Gym®. I have children achieving far higher scores than I have seen using the same screening and testing methods for the past six years. The ones who are doing Brain Gym® are accomplishing so much more."

MANDALAS AS A TOOL TO FOCUS, CALM AND GET CREATIVE

- Working from the center to the edge: Broadens attention
- Working from the edge to center: Focuses attention
- Relaxes the body
- Activates the Right Brain
- Visual Prompt/structural map for writing feelings in a poem, song or composition
- "Tilt the brain so language comes out differently" –Caryn Mirriam-Goldberg author of "Write Where you are" Free Spirit Press

A source for mandalas can be found at http://www.mandali.com/

COLOR YOUR OWN MANDALA

Sample from Monique Mandali , Everyone's Mandala Coloring Book, http://www.mandali.com/

Reading Comprehension Strategy

ENGLISH – MAPPING IT OUT[2]

What is it?
A technique that helps students understand a sequence of events in a novel/story. It can also be used to help trace the development of a character throughout the arc of a story.

In what type of "classroom setting" does this occur?
I have used this with my English classes, which were all college preparatory high school students. ***Approximately 30% of my students had an I.E.P. (Individual Education Plan) that would address their particular learning disabilities and modifications.*** This assignment was a successful learning tool for all of my students regardless of ability.

In my classroom, students work in groups of four at large tables. They remain in these groups throughout a complete unit. In other words, when we began reading Charles Dickens' *A Tale of Two Cities,* students were moved into a new group of four and would remain with this group until the novel was completed.

When we read a novel, students each keep an individual reading journal. This journal is a place where each student keeps a record of her interaction with the text. The student records the sequence of events, copies down passages that interested/puzzled her, writes down any connections she makes to other texts as well as any connection she makes between the text and herself. She also writes down any questions that occurred to her while she was reading.

Each day in class, students share with the group, as well as with the class as a whole, their reading journal entries. The class and group discussions are guided by questions that students wrote in their journals as well as open-ended questions posed by me. The primary goal of my questions is to prompt students to return to their journals and the text to discover the answers for themselves. My role as the teacher is to be the person who provides tools for discovery. I do not want to be the person who spouts information that is simply copied down and then repeated verbatim on a test.

Telling students to "Map It Out".
When we encounter an especially difficult part of the novel, I take out the crayons, markers, and newsprint. I give each group one piece of paper and an ample supply of crayons/markers. I then ask the students to map out the sequence of events in a specific part of the novel, such as Chapter 6. Each picture/image they create must be accompanied by a passage from the text. These groupings of images/text must be arranged in a sequence. Once the mapping is complete, each group will have to "read" their map to the class.

What special materials are needed?
-Crayons, art pencils, markers
-Newsprint or other type of large paper preferably white
How much class time does this typically take?

---

[2] Copyright 2000 by Liz Juster, Londonderry High School. Reprinted with Permission

Timing is related to the amount of text that students must "map out". The assignment typically takes one class period (45 min.) to map and one period to present to the other groups.

How is this assessed?

I will give each student credit equal to one homework assignment for the engagement in and completion of this project. This also allows me to meet, albeit briefly, with each student at the group table. I can then get an accurate understanding of who is doing their reading and completing their reading journals. I can also answer individual questions about the text.

A "Mapping It Out" Assignment for A Tale of Two Cities

Assignment (written on board and discussed): In the novel *A Tale of Two Cities*, Book the Second, Chapter 6 "Monseigneur in the Town" and Chapter 7 "Monseigneur in the Country", map out the events that happen to Monsieur the Marquis from the moment when he leaves the fancy party in the city until he arrives at his home in the country. You must have at least four events and a passage from the text to go with each event.

Participation Strategies

1. Ask questions that all students can answer by raising their hands high! "How many of you…?"

2. Use the Finger Count technique:

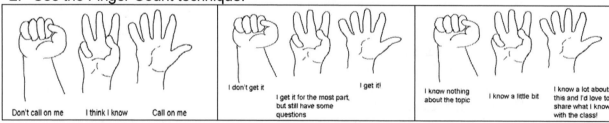

3. Have students answer questions as a "chorus" all together. "Choral Answers"

4. Use marker boards to encourage participation:
   Every student has a
   - Whiteboard
   - Dry-erase marker or wipe off crayon
   - Little kid sock (for wiping and storing marker or crayon)
     1. Teacher asks a question.
     2. Students write answers on white boards.
     3. After fair amount of time, teacher asks students to hold up boards.
   - The teacher can see how ALL students are doing in one look across the room.
   - It stops blurters.
   - Allows those that need processing time to finally get it!

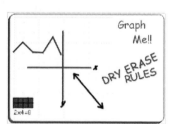

Writing Strategies

BREAKING REPORTS DOWN TO THE WRITING PROCESS

I used the form on the next page to teach students how to summarize what they read. Plagiarism is a major problem for students with learning disabilities. Their intent is seldom to "steal"; rather, they simply do not know how to summarize.

The form breaks the process of research and summarization down into a step-by-step process. The key to student success is to have them go through this process several times a semester. I had them start a new one as soon as one was finished. We always had one in process. The other **very** important component of this process is teacher review, guidance and instruction every step of the way. This process was painstakingly slow. I did a little of it in class every single day.

In order to help the students effectively, I had to read the articles they chose. I also had to help them summarize each paragraph in one sentence in the beginning. When each student is reading a different article, this is tough, however, I believed in what I was doing. The results were amazing. By the end of the semester, every single student in my class could take a standard magazine article, read it, and summarize it.

Tip:
Have the students choose more than one article. Students may pick articles that are way above their heads. It is important that they have a chance for success and an article from *The New Yorker* is probably not at the appropriate reading level for some of the students. Yes, I had students choose from that magazine! Use tact in explaining to students why they should use a 'different' article. This should not be a degrading exercise.

Or

Choose ten articles for the class and students can pick one of the ten. This is also more manageable for the teacher.

NAME_____TODAY'S DATE:_____

ENGLISH PAPER REQUIREMENTS   DUE DATE: _____

☐ Choose your topic:

My topic is: _____

☐ Use the library research, computer, or READER'S GUIDE to find an article.
☐ Attach 4 possible article listings from the Reader's Guide or computer printout.
☐ Choose 1 article.
The article must be longer than 1 full-page of print, and less than 3 full pages of print.

My choice is: Magazine_____

                  Issue date: _____

                  Article title: _____

                  Page number (s): _____

                  Author's name: _____

☐ ATTACH A COPY OF THE ARTICLE TO THIS SHEET!
☐ Write a one (1) sentence summary of each paragraph in the article.

                  Submit for proofing: Date_____ Teacher initials: _____

☐ Write a rough draft of your summary of the article AND include a paragraph stating YOUR
        THOUGHTS on the article.

                  Submit for proofing: Date_____ Teacher initials: _____

☐ Write a final Draft.

ITEM GRADED	POSSIBLE POINTS	EARNED POINTS
Reader's Guide Reference		
Copy of article		
Paragraph Summary		
Rough Draft		
Final Draft		

STRATEGY FOR GETTING "UN-STUCK" WHILE WRITING: CLUSTERING

The clustering activity detailed on the following pages helps students who are struggling to write an essay as well as young adults filling out college applications.

Clustering Activity Step One

a. If your child has to write a paper, instruct him/her to draw a big circle on a piece of paper.
b. Put the topic of the paper in the center of the circle. Note: If there is more than one topic, you might have more than one circle: Writing about three wishes will require three circles: One for each wish.
c. Instruct your child to write any thoughts, ideas, and feelings about the topic in the circle. One can also ask questions about the topic or draw pictures of ideas.
d. Do not worry about spelling, grammar, sentences, etc. at this point. The purpose is to get the ideas out. Worry about writing rules later.

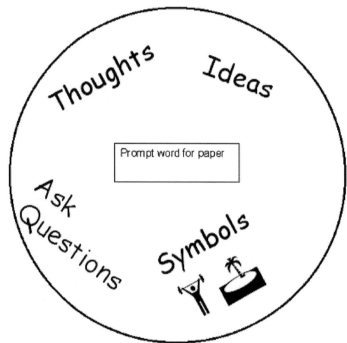

Make this circle BIG. At least the size of an 8" X 8" piece of paper.

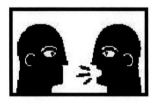

e. After students "create" in the circle, allow them to share what they have written with a partner.

Clustering Step Two

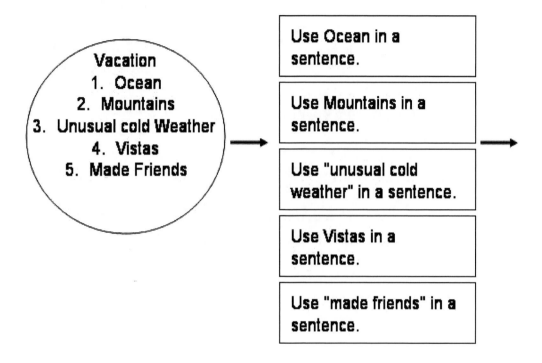

a. Instruct students to take the "best" words and ideas from inside their circle and use each word in a sentence.

b. This is the topic sentence for the paragraphs they will write.

c. Write the sentences on strips of lined notepaper or lined sticky Post It notes.

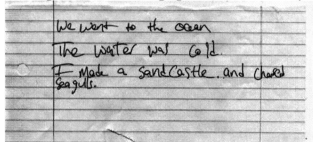

Clustering Step Three

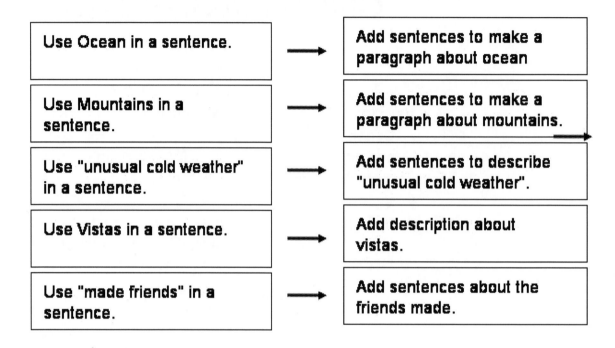

Use Ocean in a sentence. →	Add sentences to make a paragraph about ocean
Use Mountains in a sentence. →	Add sentences to make a paragraph about mountains.
Use "unusual cold weather" in a sentence. →	Add sentences to describe "unusual cold weather".
Use Vistas in a sentence. →	Add description about vistas.
Use "made friends" in a sentence. →	Add sentences about the friends made.

a. Now, take each sentence and add some more sentences about the topic sentence on that strip of paper.

b. Try to write two or three more sentences about the topic sentence.

*NOTE: Do not worry about spelling, grammar, or punctuation at this point in the exercise. Worrying about the rules makes it more difficult to be creative.

Clustering Step Four

Add sentences to make a paragraph about ocean	
Add sentences to make a paragraph about mountains.	
Add sentences to describe "unusual cold weather".	Add
Add description about vistas.	
Add sentences about the friends made.	

Add Introduction

Add Conclusion

Next, add an introduction and conclusion on separate strips of lined paper.

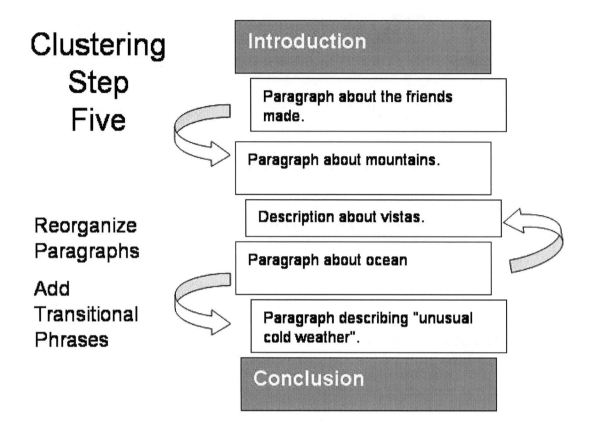

Clustering Step Five

Reorganize Paragraphs

Add Transitional Phrases

Introduction

Paragraph about the friends made.

Paragraph about mountains.

Description about vistas.

Paragraph about ocean

Paragraph describing "unusual cold weather".

Conclusion

a. Next, move the strips of paper around so that the paper is in the best order and makes the most sense.
b. This process allows the writer to start anywhere in the paper. It frees up creative thought and encourages the process to start. Organizing the paper after paragraphs are written is easy.
c. Scotch tape all the strips on one or two big pieces of paper.
d. Add transition words to make the paragraphs flow together.

Examples of Transition Words:

To Add:
And, again, and then, besides, equally important, finally, further, furthermore, nor, too, next, lastly, what's more, moreover, in addition, first (second, etc.)

To Compare:
Whereas, but, yet, on the other hand, however, nevertheless, on the other hand, on the contrary, by comparison, where, compared to, up against, balanced against, but, although, conversely, meanwhile, after all, in contrast, although this may be true

To Prove:
Because, for, since, for the same reason, obviously, evidently, furthermore, moreover, besides, indeed, in fact, in addition, in any case, that is

To Show Exception:
Yet, still, however, nevertheless, in spite of, despite, of course, once in a while, sometimes

To Show Time:
Immediately, thereafter, soon, after a few hours, finally, then, later, previously, formerly, first (second, etc.), next, and then

To Repeat:
In brief, as I have said, as I have noted, as has been noted

To Emphasize:
definitely, extremely, obviously, in fact, indeed, in any case, absolutely, positively, naturally, surprisingly, always, forever, perennially, eternally, never, emphatically, unquestionably, without a doubt, certainly, undeniably, without reservation

To Show Sequence:
First, second, third, and so forth. A, B, C, and so forth. next, then, following this, at this time, now, at this point, after, afterward, subsequently, finally, consequently, previously, before this, simultaneously, concurrently, thus, therefore, hence, next, and then, soon

To Give an Example:
For example, for instance, in this case, in another case, on this occasion, in this situation, take the case of, to demonstrate, to illustrate, as an illustration, to illustrate

To Summarize or Conclude:
In brief, on the whole, summing up, to conclude, in conclusion, as I have shown, as I have said, hence, therefore, accordingly, thus, as a result, consequently, on the whole

---

Clustering Step Six

Rewrite or type into one continuous draft on full sheets of paper.

Hand in draft for teacher to correct.

Introduction
Paragraph about the friends made.
Paragraph about mountains.
Description about vistas.
Paragraph about ocean
Paragraph describing "unusual cold weather".
Conclusion

If the teacher is not correcting a draft, you might help your child with this step.

Clustering Step Seven

Student writes final draft incorporating teacher corrections, feedback and edits.

> **My Vacation**
>
> **By Successful Student**
>
> **Interesting new friends became the focal point of ….**
>
> **The mountains were…**
>
> **The vistas were inspiring as mountains met the ocean in a clash of green and aquamarine…**
>
> **Unfortunately there was an unusual cold weather front….**
>
> **Overall, the vacation was…**

This is the place where the student uses the rules and makes sure that spelling, grammar and punctuation are correct.

Goal Setting: A Proven Motivational Strategy

Goal setting is a planning process that empowers students to take control of their progress and work toward something in which they have invested. Students need to choose their own goals. We might guide them in the process, however, if they are to be motivated to work towards the goals, they have to feel ownership.

Long-term goals are good for the big picture; however, they seldom seem to keep students motivated on a day-to-day basis. Short-term goals that work toward the long-term goal seem to keep students on task and allow them to see the milestones accomplished.

Encourage students to commit to realistic and reachable short-term goals. If students are unrealistic, they will fail to reach their goal and thus defeat the process of goal setting. It is important for students meet their goals to feel successful and not repeat a cycle of failure.

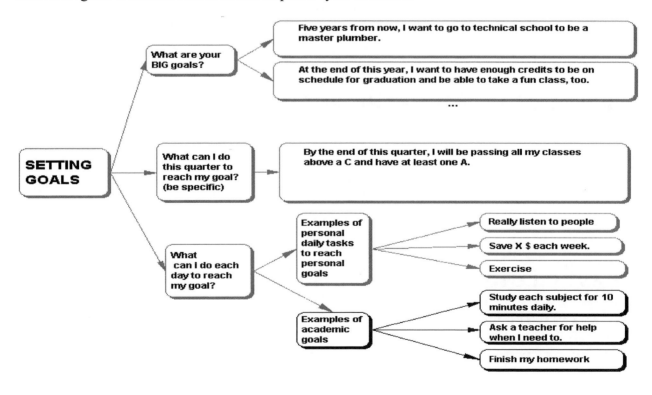

REACH FOR THE STARS
(An Experience in setting goals)

Today's date_____

THREE THINGS I WILL DO THIS QUARTER (GOALS):

    1. _____

    2. _____

    3. _____

Place a star by the most important ★ **one**

OBSTACLES TO OVERCOME:

    1. _____

    2. _____

    3. _____

HOW I WILL OVERCOME THE OBSTACLES:

_____

_____

_____

WAS I ABLE TO MEET MY GOAL (S)? _____

IF NOT, WHY NOT?

_____

_____

Win-Win Discipline Plan

NAME: _____   DATE: _____

What were you doing that was unacceptable? _____

_____

Was your behavior against the rules of the class or the school? _____ Explain: _____

_____

Was your behavior helping you?_____Explain: _____

_____

Was your behavior helping your teacher?_____Explain: _____

_____

Are you willing to try a different behavior? _____
What could you have done differently in **this** situation? _____

_____

What is your plan to follow the rules of the class (or school)? What will you change or
improve? List things you **will do** rather than things you will not do. Be specific.

_____

_____

_____

Are you willing to *accept* your plan and *stick with it?* _____

List the consequences for not following through on your plan.

_____

_____

Signatures:

_____

Student : _____   Teacher: _____

PLAN REVIEW DATE: _____   Follow up notes

_____

_____

GUIDELINES FOR DISCUSSION: WIN-WIN DISCIPLINE PLAN[1]

Questions to be addressed:

What is the Problem? Or What were you doing that was unacceptable?
In Reality Therapy, the real question is "What is the Problem?" I found this question led to an answer like, "There's no problem!" For me, "What were you doing that was unacceptable?" is a more direct, less vague and more productive question. The purpose here is to list the specific behaviors that are causing the problem. Try to avoid confronting values, attitudes, and cultural beliefs.

Whose expectations are not being met?
This question is not on the plan, but it needs to be a part of the discussion. If it is the student's own expectations, you might start with, "I'm concerned..." If it is the parent or teacher's expectations regarding rules, etc., state, "Part of my job as a (parent/teacher) is to mention... or ...to keep you safe... or ...to create a safe environment...etc. If the problem involves others' expectations, you might say, "I'm hearing things that concern me, and I want..."

What do you want as a result of the conversation?
State what you want as a result of the discussion. Word what you want in the form of a solution. "I want to work out a way that 'X' happens..." or "I want to figure out a way that we both win, ... that you get _____ and I get _____. Do not get sucked into arguing about the problem. Kids are experts at avoiding responsibility and resolution by bantering, badgering, blaming and 'Yeah, but...!'"

What will the resolution include?
The resolution might include 1) a plan for the future, 2) No plan (just a sharing of feelings, or 3) If there is a plan...a) logical consequences, or, b) no consequences. The plan must include a commitment. If it doesn't, then a new plan must be worked out that the child can commit to.

Note: When children are resistant to planning, I simply tell them that they will continue with time-out (whether that means consecutive detentions, discussions, time-outs, internal suspensions, etc.) until we 'work it out' and create a plan that we both feel comfortable with. If the plan involves restitution, it must also be acceptable to the 'victim'.

---

[1] The Win Win Discipline Plan and Guidelines are based on my experience using principles of Reality Therapy and Choice Theory. They have not been endorsed by the Institute for Reality Therapy.

EXAMPLE: ACADEMIC SUPPORT RULES AND PROCEDURES

In order to ensure a productive and peaceful environment in the Academic Support Lab, the Academic Support Lab students created the following class rules on the first day of school.

- COME TO CLASS PREPARED.
- RESPECT OTHERS AND RESPECT PROPERTY.
- DO THE BEST JOB YOU CAN.
- FOLLOW SCHOOL RULES.

- The Academic Support Lab teachers have agreed upon a student management system to enforce the class rules in an objective and fair way.

- Students who break class rules will be given two verbal reminders of the rule they are breaking with no additional consequence. Students start with a clean slate each day.

- The third time a rule is broken, the student will be given an after school detention to work out a way to solve the problem with the teacher. If students have transportation difficulties after school, before school detentions may be arranged.

- If the behavior is disruptive, the student will **also** be asked to leave the room for 5 minutes. The student will report to the assistant principal's office with a special 5-minute pass. During that time, it is hoped that the student can calm down and prepare mentally to return to class and work quietly.

- If the student returns to class, and is disruptive again, he or she will be asked to leave the class and go to his or her assistant principal's office. A demerit referral will be written. THE STUDENT STILL MUST SHOW FOR DETENTION REGARDLESS OF ADDITIONAL ADMINISTRATIVE ACTION.

- The purpose of the detention is to problem solve, providing an opportunity for the student and teacher to work together. Without this communication between the student and the teacher, problems are likely to persist.

- Students who are assigned detentions must come up with a plan to improve their success in the Academic Support Lab. If after one forty-five minute detention, they have refused to cooperate, they must stay for additional detentions until both teacher and student agree upon an acceptable plan.

- ON the other-hand, if a student comes up with a plan to work out the problem in the first 10 minutes, and both the teacher and the student agree, the teacher may dismiss the student.

It is hoped that consistency and clear guidelines contribute to a successful year in the Academic Support Lab.

I have read and understand the student management system. (This is not a contract.)

Student Signature   **Date**

Parent Signature   **Date**

Caring Inclusive Community Tools

CLASSROOM MANAGEMENT CUE CARDS

1. Create your cue card to match requests and praise you frequently state in class.
2. Stick the cue card on the top corner of each student's desk. (Laminate it, use shipping tape, etc. to make it sturdy.
3. Rather than disturb the class with a verbal correction or embarrass a student with verbal praise, walk up to the student's desk:
   a. Make eye contact.
   b. Point to the picture on the card that represents what you want to say.
   c. Walk away (Do not say anything or engage in banter.)

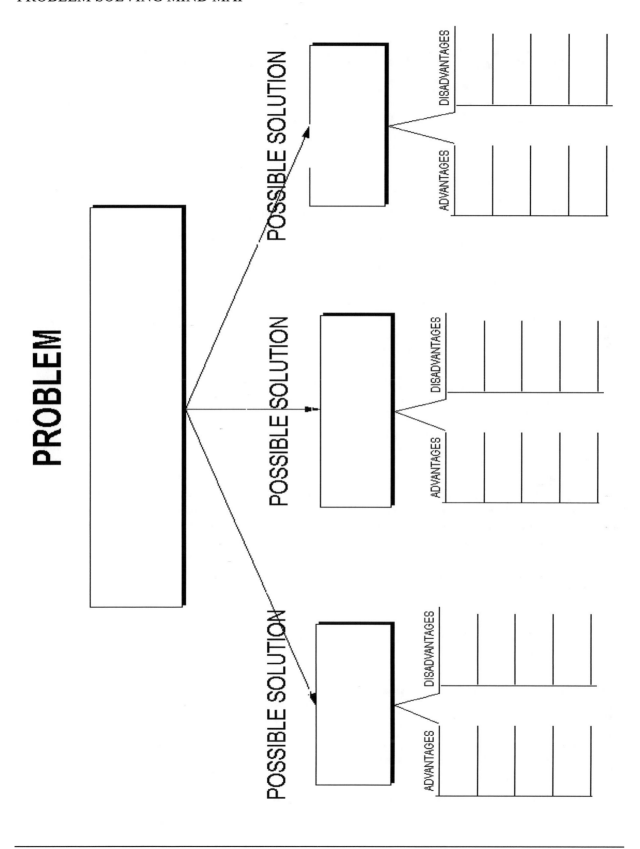

COLD WATER WORDS
A.K.A. Fogging

When you find yourself caught in a verbal exchange that does not 'feel' right, then you may be dealing with bullying-- intimidation, bulldozing, sarcasm, pushiness, exploitation, manipulation, etc.

You may, also, simply be dealing with someone who is upset over a misunderstanding and unable to communicate clearly in the moment.

First:	*RECOGNIZE & PAY ATTENTION* to your body signals — don't ignore the discomfort, adrenaline rush, etc.
Second:	*STOP, BREATHE, and THINK*: "I CAN handle this!" (Positive self-talk)
Third:	*CONCIOUSLY act*! (As opposed to Re-Act.)

Be conscious of your body language and the words you choose: <u>Keep Your Power</u>

COMMENTS

- I See
- Thank you for letting me know how you feel.
- Perhaps you are right
- I hear you
- Ouch! (Cues the other person that they are being hurtful. Sometimes they don't realize.)
- I can see this upsets you.
- I'm sorry you were hurt. That was not my intent.
- I shouldn't have to defend myself, and I won't.
- Excuse me, I'm not finished. (Say softly)
- Agree with *some* of the statement but not all. (eg. "You have a chip on your shoulder because you are short." Agree, "Yes, I am short.")
- You have an interesting perspective.
- I'll have to give that some thought.
- I will talk to you when you are calm. (Call "Time", & leave)
- I will talk to you when I am calm. (Call "Time", & leave)

ASK A QUESTION

- Why does that bother you?
- How so?
- Why do you ask?
- What makes you say that?
- I know you wouldn't have said that unless you had a good reason. Could you tell me what it was?

TIPS FOR SUCCESS

- Be careful about tone of voice
- Lower your voice
- Avoid "should", "ought", and "you" statements.
- ASK A QUESTION— S/he who asks the question has the power.

Teacher Tools: Letters and Forms

SAMPLE LETTER TO STUDENTS TO ASSIST WITH FOLLOW-UP

Monday, September 14, 2000

To:_____

From: Mrs. Fitzell, Student Services Department

Hello! I have chosen to be your case manager for this school year. I am looking forward to working with you. I am giving you a copy of my class schedule so that you may know where I can be found if you need me for anything during the school day. Please keep this somewhere in your notebook, folder or your backpack. If there are any changes, I will let you know. If you find you are having problems with class work, I will be happy to find a way to help you or get you the help you need. Just try to let me know when you will need me.

Mrs. Fitzell's Schedule

BEFORE SCHOOL:	ROOM145B
A PERIOD:	ROOM 145B or Student Services Office
B PERIOD:	ROOM 176
C PERIOD:	ROOM 176
D PERIOD	ROOM M1
E PERIOD:	LUNCH/ROOM 145B or Student Services Office
F PERIOD:	USUALLY ROOM 145B or Student Services Office
G PERIOD:	ROOM 202
H PERIOD:	ROOM 301
AFTER SCHOOL:	ROOM 145B

SAMPLE LETTER TO TEACHERS TO ASSIST WITH FOLLOW-UP

Date:

Dear _____,

_____is in your pd._____ _____class,

and has Academic Support Lab _____period. Please take a moment to fill out the information below. This will assist us greatly in helping this student to be successful in your class.

Please Circle One:

1. Estimate Grade: **A   B   C   D   F**

2. Turns in Homework: **Always   Sometimes   Never**

3. Tests/Quizzes: **High   Average   Low   Failing**

4. Do you feel this student could benefit from any ongoing remedial instruction? If yes, please explain.

5. Please list any assignments/tests that need to be made-up/completed.

Thank you for taking the time to complete this form!

Sincerely,

"QUICK FORM" LETTER TO TEACHERS TO ASSIST WITH FOLLOW-UP

Dear _____,

The following students are in your pd._____ _____class, and have Academic Support Lab. Please take a moment to fill out the information below. This will assist us greatly in helping these students to be successful in your class. Return to _____by _____.

Student Name	Est. Grade	Missing Homework?	Missing Tests/Quizzes	Assignments/Tests that need to be made-up or completed	Comments

CLASS LIST ADAPTATIONS CHART

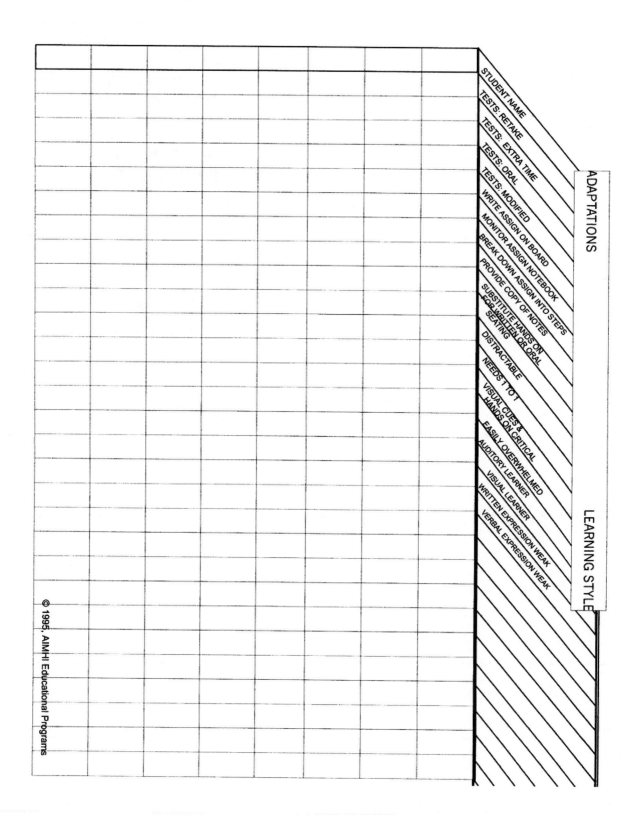

The chart has the following column headers, grouped under **ADAPTATIONS** and **LEARNING STYLE**:

STUDENT NAME

ADAPTATIONS
- TESTS: RETAKE
- TESTS: EXTRA TIME
- TESTS: ORAL
- TESTS: MODIFIED
- WRITE ASSIGN ON BOARD
- MONITOR ASSIGN NOTEBOOK
- BREAK DOWN ASSIGN INTO STEPS
- PROVIDE COPY OF NOTES
- SUBSTITUTE HANDS ON FOR WRITTEN OR ORAL
- SEATING

LEARNING STYLE
- DISTRACTABLE
- NEEDS TTOT
- VISUAL CUES & HANDS ON CRITICAL
- EASILY OVERWHELMED
- AUDITORY LEARNER
- VISUAL LEARNER
- WRITTEN EXPRESSION WEAK
- VERBAL EXPRESSION WEAK

© 1995, AIMHI Educational Programs

132   **Successful Inclusion Strategies**

CONFIDENTIAL

Student   Grade

Learning Style   Multiple Intelligence

Interests

Strengths   Challenges

Notes/Reminders:

Areas of
Concern:

Class Activity	Student Activity	Goals/Mods Met	Supports Needed

Other:

DIFFERENTIATED PLANNING: LESSON PLANNER

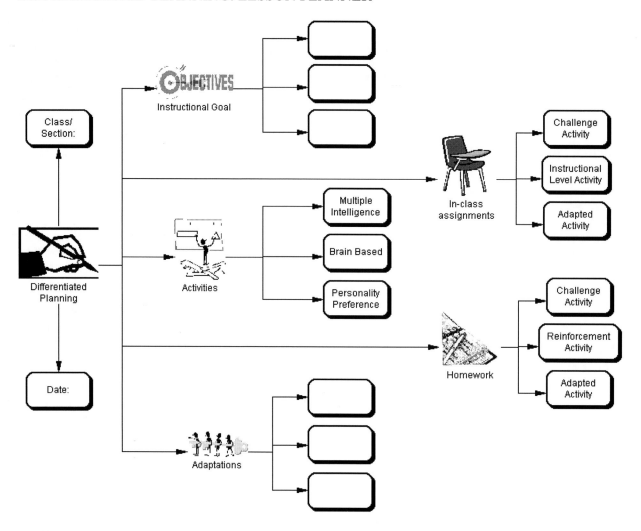

Goal:

Date	Activities	Adaptations	In-Class Assign	Homework

Assessment:

		Excuse Book	
	Please print clearly so that your parent/guardian can read your excuse.		
DATE	NAME	EXCUSE	WHAT YOU PLAN TO DO

[2] Adapted From *Current, Best Ideas for Making Inclusion Work* by Dr. Lisa Dieker

POINTS CHART

Class_____ Period_____

1 POINT FOR EACH: W = writing utensil   P = present on time
N = notebook/textbook   C = class work   B = behavior

STUDENT	MON	TUES	WED	THU	FRI	TOT
1.						
2.						
3.						
4.						
5.						
6.						
7.						
8.						
9.						
10.						
11.						
12.						
13.						
14.						
15.						
16.						
17.						
18.						
19.						
20.						
21.						
22.						
23.						
24.						
25.						
26.						
27.						
28.						

Appendix--Student Organizational Tools

Note Taking Strategies

CUT AND PASTE NOTES USING MIND MAPS AND CHARTS

Consider the graphic organizer on the following page and the different ways it can be used to differentiate:

1. Whenever you are presenting a "process", show the process visually in a process map. This will help the students to visually see what you are teaching and will enhance memory of the process.

2. Give students a process map or a graphic organizer with blank boxes.
   a. Have students fill in the key words as you teach about the topic.
   b. Give students a grid of the key words, a glue stick, and scissors. Have them cut out the words.
      i. Then as you <u>teach</u> the lesson, instruct students to move the words to the correct box and paste them down.
      ii. Then as you <u>review</u> the lesson, instruct students to move the words to the correct box and paste them down.
      iii. <u>Power of Two:</u> Instruct students to work together to decide where the words go on the map and move the words to the correct box. Teacher might review student's answers and, when correct, instruct them to paste them down.
   c. The graphic organizer can be used as a quiz or test thereby minimizing the difficulty for students who read below grade level. Students show what they know without being hindered by their reading disability.

For another excellent resource see:
Council For Exceptional Children
Archived Teaching Exceptional Children
VOL. 34 NO. 2, NOV/DEC 2001
Cut and Paste 101 - New Strategies for Note Taking and Review
Author: Lorene K. Porte, Available at the link below:
http://journals.cec.sped.org/EC/Archive_Articles/VOL.34NO.2NOVDEC2001_TEC_Article2.pdf

---

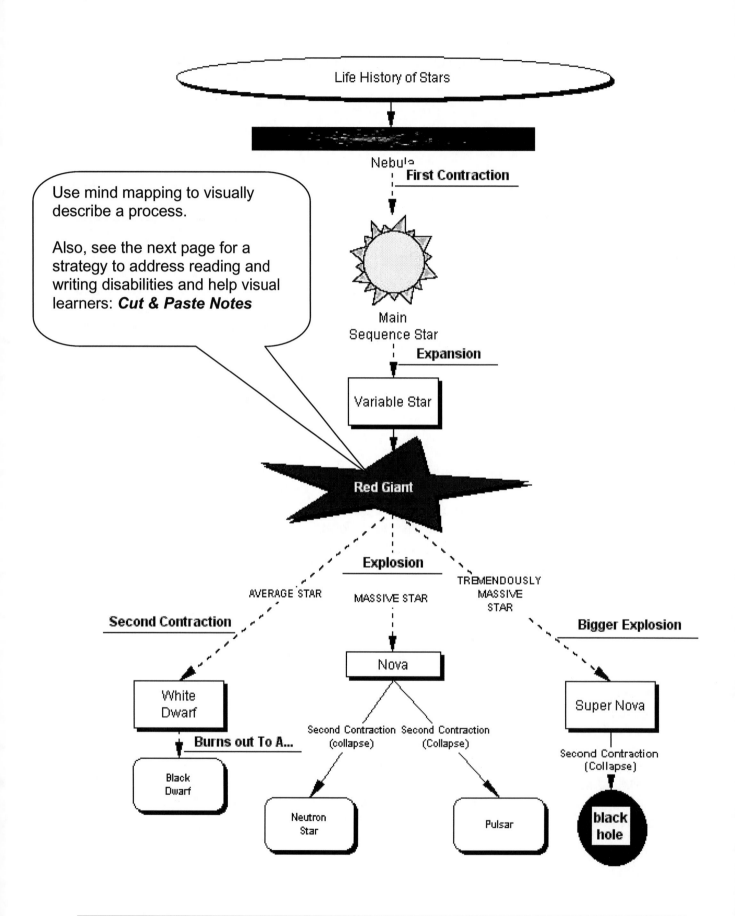

Use mind mapping to visually describe a process.

Also, see the next page for a strategy to address reading and writing disabilities and help visual learners: *Cut & Paste Notes*

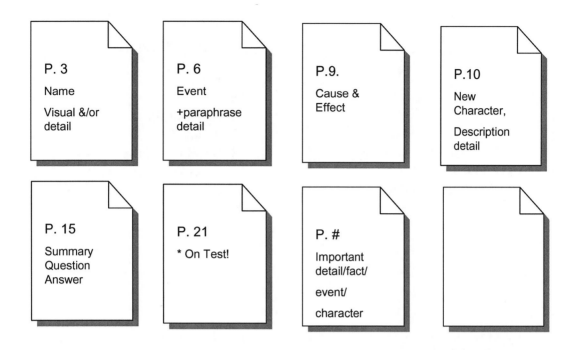

P. 3

Name

Visual &/or detail

P. 6

Event

+paraphrase detail

P.9.

Cause & Effect

P.10

New Character,

Description detail

P. 15

Summary Question Answer

P. 21

* On Test!

P. #

Important detail/fact/

event/

character

As students are reading a text, every time an important fact, item, cause and effect situation, etc., comes up, have students put a post-it note right in that spot and write the page number, the item and a visual or some detail.

After the chapter is read, the novel is finished, the text section is done, students should take all the post-it notes and line them up sequentially (as in the picture above) on a sheet of 8 ½ X 12 paper.

• Place the paper in a sleeve protector.
• Students now have a study guide that ties into the text

NOTEBOOK CHECK

Name:
Date:
[ ] Outstanding
Notebook!!
[ ] Notebook Satisfactory
[ ] Please organize your
notebook for a recheck
tomorrow.

Name:
Date:
[ ] Outstanding
Notebook!!
[ ] Notebook Satisfactory
[ ] Please organize your
notebook for a recheck
tomorrow.

Name:
Date:
[ ] Outstanding
Notebook!!
[ ] Notebook Satisfactory
[ ] Please organize your
notebook for a recheck
tomorrow.

Name:
Date:
[ ] Outstanding
Notebook!!
[ ] Notebook Satisfactory
[ ] Please organize your
notebook for a recheck
tomorrow.

Name:
Date:
[ ] Outstanding
Notebook!!
[ ] Notebook Satisfactory
[ ] Please organize your
notebook for a recheck
tomorrow.

Name:
Date:
[ ] Outstanding
Notebook!!
[ ] Notebook Satisfactory
[ ] Please organize your
notebook for a recheck
tomorrow.

In upper grades, middle schools and early high school, students need to organize their materials responsibly. Consider requiring students to keep notebooks in a specific order (See Landmark System in Appendix) and checking the notebooks weekly for the first few months of school. After that, periodic spot checks may be needed.

Adapted From *Current, Best Ideas for Making Inclusion Work* by Dr. Lisa Dieker

LANDMARK NOTEBOOK SYSTEM

The Landmark Notebook System is designed to help you keep your papers, assignments, handouts, etc. organized and in a location where you can find them should you need to refer to them again. Like any new system, it requires practice and discipline until it becomes a habit.

You will need:

- [ ] One 1" binder. You can put 1-2 subjects in one binder. (Four subjects required two binders)
- [ ] Portable three-hole punch
- [ ] Zippered pouch with holes to fit in binder
- [ ] A ruler with three holes
- [ ] 8-section dividers/binder
- [ ] Two three-hole divider pockets
- [ ] Two highlighters of different colors
- [ ] Post it notes
- [ ] Small package of skinny colored markers or gel pens
- [ ] Highlighter tape
- [ ] Pens and pencils
- [ ] Three-column notepaper
- [ ] Three hole reinforcers
- [ ] One accordion file for each subject in a binder
- [ ] Assignment calendar/notebook

Set up your binder this way:

Work from the front and arrange in the following order:
1. Three hole punch
2. Ruler
3. Zippered pouch with highlighters, writing utensils, tape, reinforcers, etc.
4. Assignment calendar
5. Divider labeled HOMEWORK
6. Divider labeled NOTES
7. Divider labeled TESTS/QUIZZES
8. Divider labeled HANDOUTS
9. Pocket divider
10. Repeat dividers for second subject

Use sections for homework, notes, tests/quizzes, handouts for one lesson chapter/unit. When the unit is finished, move ALL the papers to your accordion file for that subject and label that section with the unit name. Save the accordion file at home for midterms and final exams. Do not throw study materials away!

For more information, contact Landmark Foundation @ 508-927-4440, www.landmarkschool.org

On the next page is an effective format for note taking

THREE COLUMN NOTE PAPER

BIG IDEAS	DETAILS	TEST QUESTIONS

Successful Inclusion Strategies

Simple Sentence:

_____

Are there any words that can be made more specific?

_____

Who?	What?	When?	Where?	Why?

New improved sentence:

_____

. _____

. _____

.

Is there another way this sentence could begin?

_____

. _____

CURRENT EVENTS

Name & Date:_____

Circle one: World   Nation   Local

Do this: Find an article from a newspaper that is interesting to you.
Answer the following questions about the article. Attach the article or a
photocopy.

Cite your source: _____

Who is the story about? (Your answer could be a group of people, an
organization, or one person). _____

What event or happening does the article tell about?

_____
_____
_____
_____

Where did this event happen? (A city, a state, a building, or an area).

_____
_____

When did the event reported on in the article take place? (Time, a specific
day or date, or a reference to a time-yesterday, last week, etc.).

_____
_____

Why did the event in the article happen? (Does your story explain what
may have caused this to happen?)

_____
_____

What is your opinion about this article?

_____
_____
_____

BOOK REPORT:

Title of Book:

_____

Author:

_____

Illustrator:

_____

Publishing Co. & Place of Publication:

_____

Copyright date:

_____

Type of Story: Mystery, historical fiction, science fiction, adventure, biography

_____

TIME:

Historical period: (Medieval age, Victorian age, Early America, 1900's, etc.)

_____

Duration: (Over what period of time does the story take place? One day, several weeks, one hundred years, etc.?)

_____

PLACE:

Geographical location:

_____

Scenes: (Where does most of the story take place? Examples: outdoors, in someone's home, in a magician's castle)

_____

MAIN CHARACTER:

    Name:

_____

    Physical description:(What does he/she look like?)

_____

_____

    Personality description: (What makes him/her special?)

_____

_____

    How does this character change during the story?

_____

_____

_____

    What feelings does he/she go through?

_____

_____

_____

THE CONFLICTS IN THE STORY (The conflicts are the problems or hard decisions that the characters had to make.)

CONFLICTS/PROBLEMS	HOW DID YOUR CHARACTER DEAL WITH THE PROBLEMS?
1	

CONFLICTS/PROBLEMS	HOW DID YOUR CHARACTER DEAL WITH THE PROBLEMS?
2	

3	

TELL SOME OF THE EXCITING THINGS THAT YOUR CHARACTER DID AND HOW HIS OR HER PERSONALITY MADE THESE PARTS EXCITING.

_____

_____

_____

YOUR OPINION OF THIS STORY:

What did you like about it?

_____

What didn't you like about it?

_____

_____

PROJECT PLANNING CHART

NAME: _____

Project Topic

Date Due

I will present the project by doing...

_____ will proof read my project
(Hint: pick someone who can spell)

I will need the following materials

_____

_____

_____

I will look for information in the following places

_____

_____

_____

_____

_____

Copyright 2000 by Susan Fitzell   Created with Inspiration Software

Team Name: GRADE REVIEW SHEET   **Quarter:**

Name: **Class:**

ASSIGNMENT TITLE, DATE, GRADE	HW %	CW %	QUIZZES %	TESTS %

- **Include DATE, TITLE AND GRADE for each assignment received.**
- **This grade list should be kept in the front of your binder!**
- **Graph your grades so you can SEE how you are doing! Use a bar or line graph.**

Appendix—Lesson Prep Tools

Readability Formulas

SMOG Readability Formula

The SMOG formula is a recommended and tested method for grading the readability of written materials. The method is quick, simple to use and particularly useful for shorter materials, e.g., a study's information pamphlet or consent form. To calculate the SMOG reading level, begin with the entire written work being assessed and follow these steps:

1. Count off 10 consecutive sentences near the beginning, in the middle, and near the end of the text. If the text has fewer than 30 sentences, use as many as are provided.
2. Count the number of words containing 3 or more syllables (polysyllabic), including repetitions of the same word.
3. Look up the approximate grade level on the SMOG conversion table below:

Total Polysyllabic Word Count	Approximate Grade Level (+1.5 Grades)
1-6	5
7-12	6
13-20	7
21-30	8
31-42	9
43-56	10
57-72	11
73-90	12
91-110	13
111-132	14
133-156	15
157-182	16
183-210	17
211-240	18

For more info including Spanish formulas: http://www.cdc.gov/OD/ads/smog.htm

---

When using the SMOG formula:
A sentence is defined as a string of words punctuated with a period, an exclamation mark, or a question mark. Consider long sentences with a semi-colon as two sentences.

Hyphenated words are considered as one word.

Numbers, which are written, should be counted. If written in numeric form, they should be pronounced to determine if they are polysyllabic.

Proper nouns, if polysyllabic, should be counted.

Abbreviations should be read as though unabbreviated to determine if they are polysyllabic. However, abbreviations should be avoided unless commonly known.
If the written piece being graded is shorter than 30 sentences, approach it as follows:

Count all of the polysyllabic words in the test.
Count the number of sentences.
Find the average number of polysyllabic words per sentence, i.e.:

Total # of polysyllabic words
Average = Total # of sentences
Multiply that average by the average number of sentences *short* of 30.
Add that figure on to the total number of polysyllabic words.
Compare the number of polysyllabic words in the SMOG conversion table.

For the Fry Readability Formula see:
http://school.discovery.com/schrockguide/fry/fry.html

To display readability statistics in MSWord (These instructions are for MSWord 2000):

1. On the Tools menu, click Options, and then click the Spelling & Grammar tab.
2. Select the *Check grammar with spelling* check box.
3. Select the *Show readability statistics check box*, and then click OK.
4. Click *Spelling and Grammar* on the Standard toolbar.
5. When Word finishes checking spelling and grammar, it displays information about the reading level of the document.

IMPORTANT: Do not include word banks or word lists in readability checks. They skew the score and yield inaccurate results. Highlight sentences or paragraphs separately instead.

To reduce reading difficulty:
1. Shorten sentences
2. Choose words that have less than three syllables to convey the same meaning as a multi-syllabic word.

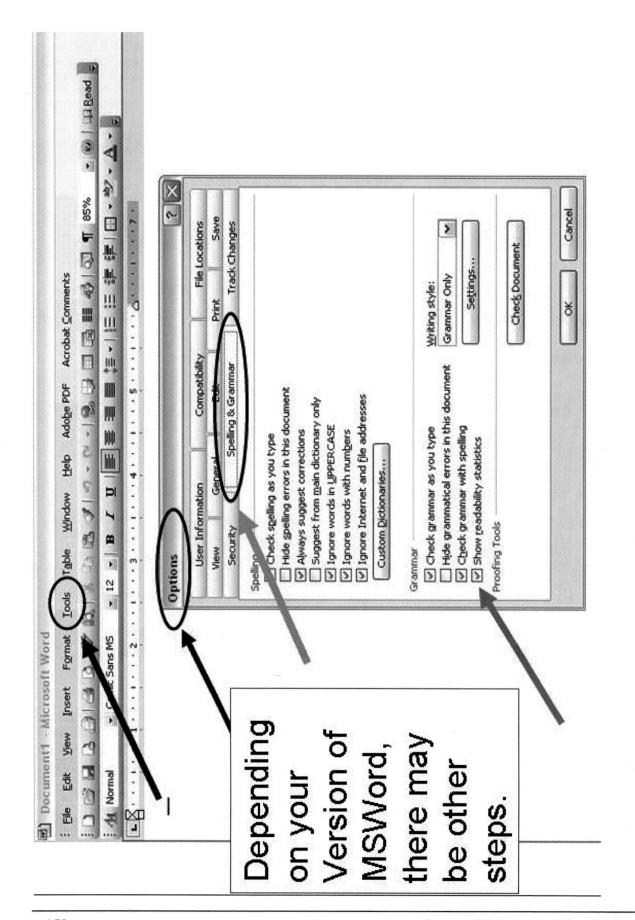

Depending on your version of MSWord, there may be other steps.

AutoSummarize in MSWord

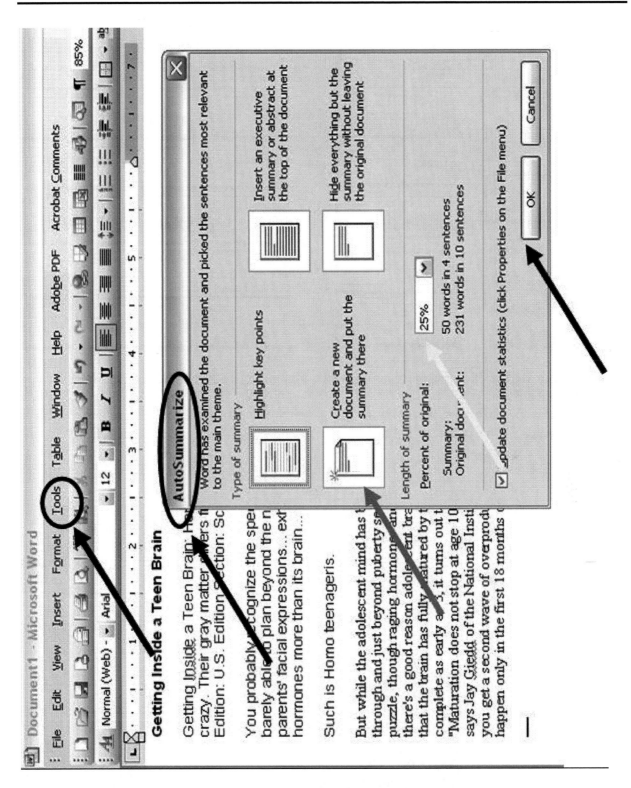

Tip: When copying from the Internet into MSWord, instead of using "Paste" use "Paste Special" and paste as "formatted text" or "unformatted text".

Bloom's Taxonomy & Questioning Technique

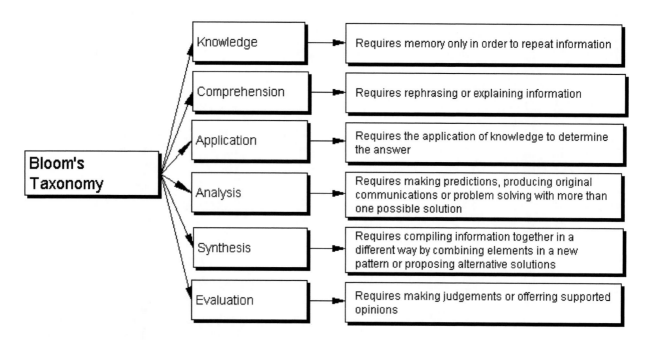

Level 1: Knowledge - exhibits previously learned material by recalling facts, terms, basic concepts, and answers.

Key words: who, what, why, when, omit, where, which, choose, find, how, define, label, show, spell, list, match, name, relate, tell, recall, select

Questions:

What is . . . ? How is . . . ? Where is . . . ? When did _____ happen? How did _____ happen? How would you explain . . . ? Why did . . . ? How would you describe . . . ?

Level 2: Comprehension - demonstrating understanding of facts and ideas by organizing, comparing, translating, interpreting, giving descriptions, and stating main ideas.

Key words: compare, contrast, demonstrate, interpret, explain, extend, illustrate, infer, outline, relate, rephrase, translate, summarize, show, classify

Questions:

How would you classify the type of . . . ? How would you compare . . . ? contrast . . . ? Will you state or interpret in your own words . . . ? What is the main idea of . . . ?

Level 3: Application - solving problems by applying acquired knowledge, facts, techniques, and rules in a different way.

Key words: apply, build, choose, construct, develop, interview, make use of, organize, experiment with, plan, select, solve, utilize, model, identify

Questions:

How would you use . . . ? What examples can you find to . . . ? How would you solve ____ using what you have learned . . . ? How would you organize _____ to show . . . ? How would you show your understanding of . . . ? What approach would you use to . . . ?

Level 4: Analysis - examining and breaking information into parts by identifying motives or causes; making inferences and finding evidence to support generalizations.

Key words: analyze, categorize, classify, compare, contrast, discover, dissect, divide, examine, inspect, simplify, survey, take part in, test for, distinguish, list, distinction, theme, relationships, function, motive, inference, assumption, conclusion

Questions:
What are the parts or features of . . . ? How is _____ related to . . . ? Why do you think . . . ? What is the theme . . . ? What motive is there . . . ? Can you list the parts . . . ? What inference can you make . . . ?

Level 5: Synthesis - compiling information together in a different way by combining elements in a new pattern or proposing alternative solutions.

Key Words: build, choose, combine, compile, compose, construct, create, design, develop, estimate, formulate, imagine, invent, make up, originate, plan, predict, propose, solve, solution, suppose, discuss, modify, change, original, improve, adapt, minimize, maximize, delete, theorize, elaborate, test, improve, happen, change

Questions:
What changes would you make to solve . . . ? How would you improve . . . ? What would happen if . . . ? Can you elaborate on the reason . . . ? Can you propose an alternative . . . ? Can you invent . . . ? How would you adapt _____ to create a different . . . ?

Level 6: Evaluation - presenting and defending opinions by making judgments about information, validity of ideas or quality of work based on a set of criteria.

Key Words: award, choose, conclude, criticize, decide, defend, determine, dispute, evaluate, judge, justify, measure, compare, mark, rate, recommend, rule on, select, agree, interpret, explain, appraise, prioritize, opinion, ,support, importance, criteria, prove, disprove, assess, influence, perceive, value, estimate, influence, deduct

Questions:
Do you agree with the actions . . . ? with the outcomes . . . ? What is your opinion of . . . ? How would you prove . . . ? disprove . . . ? Can you assess the value or importance of . . . ? Would it be better if . . . ? Why did they (the character) choose . . . ? What would you recommend . . . ?

Reference: *Quick Flip Questions for Critical Thinking*, based on Bloom's Taxonomy developed by Linda G. Barton

Adapted from *Bloom's Taxonomy and Critical Thinking* by Barbara Fowler, Longview Community College http://www.kcmetro.cc.mo.us/longview/ctac/blooms.htm

Appendix –Quick Reference Lists

Social Studies Adaptations

Decorate the classroom with students' drawings of the culture being studied.	Make an historical comic strip that meets specific criteria.
Compile a notebook of history jokes. Work facts into the jokes.	Play charades with "significant" events from the unit you are studying.
Create history raps that identify key dates and people.	Play 'What's my line?" or "Pictionary" with names, dates, places.
Create time sequence charts with titles for major eras of history-- then create a mnemonic out of the sequence of the titles.	Write a skit or play from a period in history, or as a typical day in a specific culture. Example: Sparta or Athens.
Make a game of predicting what will happen in several current event stories.	Play "guess the culture" based on artifacts in a time capsule.
Debate important issues and decisions from the past.	Play charades with "significant" events from the unit you are studying.
Create limericks about important historical events.	Role-play a conversation with an important historical figure.
Have students conduct imaginary interviews with people from the past.	Write a skit or play from a period in history, or as a typical day in a specific culture. Example: Sparta or Athens.
Have students draw a mural that reflects a specific time period.	Generate an illustration which best depicts what democracy* means to you. (Engages brain to store data.) *Example.
Role-play a conversation with an important historical figure.	Make visual diagrams and flow charts of historical information.
Make maps out of salt dough and show geographical features and key places.	Send a post card from one historical character to another historical character.

English/Language Arts/Foreign Language Adaptations

Teach "concept mapping" to help remember content or take notes.	Create song rap to teach grammar and syntax.
Write a sequel/next episode to a story or play.	Use different kinds of music for different kinds of writing.
Create crossword puzzles/word jumbles for vocabulary words.	Analyze literature for "connections to our lives today."
Practice impromptu speaking and writing.	Predict what will happen next in a story or play.
Experiment with joint story-writing- one starts then pass it on.	Analyze a story and describe its message-reach a consensus.
Use a "human graph" to see where a group stands on an issue.	Analyze similarities and differences of various pieces of literature.
Use a "story grid" for creative writing activities.	Read poetry from different perspectives and in different moods.
Play vocabulary words "Pictionary."	Conduct language drill exercises with partner.
Draw pictures of the different stages of a story you are reading.	Write an autobiographical essay: My life to date, my life in the future.
Use highlight markers to "colorize" parts of a story or poem. (Option: Highlight tape.)	Write a new poem each day of the week on "Who am I."
Use sticky notes to make predictions as you read a story or novel.	Imagine being a character in a story/play-what would you do.
Write a letter to the author telling him/her how well you liked (or didn't like) his/her book.	

Math Adaptations

Write a series of story problems for others to solve.	Learn mathematical operations through songs and jingles, rhythm.
Explain how to work a problem to others while they follow.	Use a formula card for tests.
Make up puns using math vocabulary or terms.	Provide tables, graph paper, lines and space for working problems.
Solve problems with a partner: 1 solves and 1 explains process.	Make up sounds for different math operations and processes.
Create poems telling when to use different math operations.	Solve complex story problems in a group.
Teach how to use a calculator for problem solving.	Do a statistical research project and calculate percentages.
Create number sequences and have a partner find the pattern.	"Each one teach one" new math processes/operations.
Mind-map proofs for geometry theorems.	Describe everything you do to solve a problem to a partner.
Design classification charts for math formulas and operations.	Have teams construct problems linking many math operations, then solve them.
Do a survey of students' likes/dislikes then graph the results.	Track thinking patterns for different math problems.
Estimate measurements by sight and by touch.	Bridge math concepts beyond school. (What? So what? Now what?)
Add, subtract, multiply, and divide using manipulatives.	Imagine using a math process successfully, then really do it.
Learn metric measurement through visual equivalents.	

Practical Arts & P.E. Adaptations

Give verbal explanation of sport routines.	Have students imagine the computer is human-draw how it works.
Have students tell another how to run a word processing program – then do it.	Have students perform physical exercise routines in sync with music.
Have students pretend they are a radio sportscasters describing a game in progress.	Play "Recipe Jeopardy" – make questions for answers given.
Use music to help improve keyboarding skills and speed.	Teach and play a series of non-competitive games.
Use peer coaching teams for individual shop projects.	Assign teams to prepare and serve meals from foreign countries.
Have students draw pictures of how to perform certain physical feats.	Have students work in pairs to learn and improve sports skills.
Teach a series of "spatial games" (e.g. horseshoes, ring toss).	Create cooperative computing teams to learn computer skills.
Create visual diagrams of how to use shop machines.	Have students list how things learned in shop can help in your future life.
Teach students to imagine a skill and then try to do it exactly as they imagined.	Capture process involved in art or sport on video or camera and create a step-by-step manual using the images.
Capture process involved in art or sport on video or camera and create review materials using the images.	Choose Textbooks with CD Rom companion.

Science and Health Adaptations

Write a humorous story using science vocabulary.	Group research projects-Groups design and implement plans.
Create a diary on "The Life of a Red Blood Cell."	Use lab teams for science experiments and exercises.
Write steps used in an experiment so someone else can do it.	Discuss controversial health topics and write team position papers.
Making up an imaginary conversation between parts of the body.	Describe the "before and after" of key scientific paradigm shifts.
Give a speech on "Ten steps to healthful living."	Learn the pattern of successful and reliable scientific experiments.
Use the symbols of the Period Table of Elements in a story.	Practice webbing attributes of various systems of the body.
Find five different ways to classify a collection of leaves.	Draw pictures of things seen under a microscope.
Create montages/collages on science topics (e.g., mammals).	Create posters/flyers Showing health processes.
Use vocabulary games to study, & review science vocabulary.	Use concrete models to demonstrate science concepts, parts.
Use concrete models as metaphors for systems in the human body.	Use Forensic science activities to create interest in scientific method, research, etc.

Differentiated Instruction Quick List

A Teaching Model for Academic Diversity & Talent Development: Flexible Grouping

Continual Assessment and Adaptation	
Foundational / Transformational Information, Ideas, Materials, Applications	*Smaller Leap / Greater Leap* Application, Insight, Transfer
Concrete / Abstract Representations, Ideas, Applications, Materials	*More Structured / More Open* Solution, Design, Monitoring
Simple / Complex Resources, Research, Issues, Problems, Skills, Goals	*Slower / Quicker* Pace of Study, Pace of Thought
Single Faceted / Multi-Faceted Disciplinary Connections, Directions	

Content	Process	Product
▪ Concept & Generalization Based ▪ High Relevance	▪ Concept & Generalization Driven ▪ Focused ▪ High Level ▪ Purposeful	▪ Concepts/Issue Centered ▪ Teach skills for planning ▪ Teach skills for production ▪ Requires application of all key skills and disciplines ▪ Uses Real Problems / Audiences ▪ Offers Multiple Modes of Expression
<u>Differentiation Through:</u> Multiple tests & supplementary print resources Varied computer programs Audio visuals Varied support mechanisms Varied time allotments Interest centers Contracts	**<u>Differentiation Through:</u>** Tiered assignments Learning centers Multiple Intelligence type assignments Graphic organizers Concept development Brain based techniques Learning style considerations	**<u>Differentiation Through:</u>** Tiered product assignments Independent study Community based assignments Negotiated criteria Graduated Rubrics MI-Based orientations Learning style considerations

Adapted from http://siksik.learnnet.nt.ca/ECE/ecss/school/support/2/html/diffinst.htm (Tomlinson)

Difficulty /Adaptation Quick List

DIFFICULTY	ADAPTATION
Poor literacy skills	Provide simpler text/use peer support.
Speech/language difficulty	Check understanding of key words Partner/group oral work.
Listening/following instructions	Highlight/cue in to important information/provide lists.
Poor numeric skills	Provide apparatus e.g. counters, algebra manipulatives.
Written work: copying notes, taking notes from lecture, etc.	Use alternative forms of recording.
Grasping/retaining new concepts	Give more practice. Use smaller steps. Use alternative language. Use memory strategies.
Difficulty with maps/graphs/charts	Tracing Photocopy. Copy and enlarge, add color/shading.
Short concentration span/keeping on task	Provide short tasks, frequent verbal cues.
Distracts others/is distracted	Sit in front, isolate from others, explore supportive groups.
Working independently	Pair with responsible partner.
Keeping classroom code of conduct	Give positive reinforcement. Diary of specific incidents.
Relating to other pupils	Change seating position or group. Monitor triggers.
Working in cooperation with others	Pair with responsible partner. Define group rules.
Relating positively to adults	Be a role model. Negotiate one to one.
Slow pace work	Realistic deadlines. Allow extra time.
Handwriting/presentation difficulties	Allow extra time and/or alternative ways of recording.
Low self-esteem/lack of confidence	Notice positives. Plan for success/achievement, give classroom responsibilities.
Organizational skills	Encourage use of lists, routines, labels, study buddies.
Homework	Time to explain homework in lesson. Time for class to record assignment. Use parental support.
Becoming upset at difficulties	Notice Positives. Reassure.

Adaptation Quick List

- White Out Method –Create fill-ins from handouts with white-out
- Achievement Award –Give awards for non-standard achievement. Use as a motivator.
- Modify Format
    - Enlarge
    - Simplify
    - Structure
    - Sequence
    - Chart
    - Pictures
    - Concrete models
    - Crosswords for review
    - Books on tape
    - Markerboard (flash answers in a group)
    -
- Memory Aides
    - Clues
    - Color code
    - Silly ditty
    - Visuals
    - Word box
    - Memory map
    - Flow chart process
    - Mnemonics
    - Evoke emotion
    - Make it meaningful vs. by the book
    - Color + (print vs. cursive) + black or blue Ink
    - Picture story, directions, process vs. list + lecture
- Adapt
    - Reword
    - Hands-on
    - Outline
    - Highlight Key points
    - Mini-post it notes
    - From word lists on paper to index cards
    - Lower reading level resources
- Other
    - Learning Style Techniques – See Appendix – How To
    - Multiple Intelligence Techniques– See Appendix – How To
    - Brain Based Learning -— See Appendix – How To

Sample I.E.P. Pages

Following are examples of how to attach adaptations & modifications to the I.E.P.

Student Name: Dominic Seymour	Grade:7
Auditory Processing, Sp. & Language	Case Coordinator: Susan Fitzell

Strengths
Avg. Intelligence, athletic, working with hands, artistic, musically inclined

Area where student will experience most difficulty
- Word retrieval
- Limited vocabulary: sticks to words he can spell, limits vocab. use
- Communicating with adults and peers
- Remembering material presented through lecture
- Making connections
- Testing
- Abstract reasoning: needs concrete—very literal

Classroom adaptations
- Provide word bank to use in short answer or fill-in-the-blank items.
- Consider crosswords for testing and review.
- Use/Teach use of graphic organizers.
- Allow extra time for response when asking a question.
- Show models of material being taught, assignments required.
- Use visual and graphic cues whenever possible.
- Consider graphic organizers on tests.
- Teach memorization strategies.
- Encourage use of rap, chants, music to commit material to memory.
- When introducing ideas use clear, simple, concrete language.
- Require that Dominic speak and write in complete sentences.
- Work in small groups encouraging Dominic to talk.
- Use index cards to review sequential material.
- Disregard mechanical errors when not learning mechanics.
- Give Dominic the opportunity to correct mechanical errors before final grading.
- Encourage and provide opportunities for peer review and practice.
- Teach new material in small chunks.

Student Name: Mary Wiley	**Grade:** 9
Emotional /Behavioral Difficulty	**Case Coordinator:** Susan Fitzell

Strengths
Above average intelligence, energetic, outgoing, creative

Area where student will experience most difficulty
- Transitions
- Adapting to different methods of classroom organization
- Adapting to different teacher styles
- Focusing on task
- Accepting boundaries for behavior
- Listening and attention skills
- Controlling reactions
- Picking up on facial expressions and body language

Classroom adaptations
- Greet Mary as she enters the classroom.
- Praise vs. Disapproval 3:1.
- Have high expectations.
- Cue her to refocus and get back on task.
- Provide and/or help her set up organization checklists.
- Mary responds best to a calm, structured and authoritative discipline approach.
- Use behavior plans with Mary when appropriate.
- Establish eye contact when speaking with Mary.
- Provide Mary with a warning/cue before transitions and change.
- Use feelings poster when working one on one with Mary to discuss her emotion and that of others.
- Develop a close liaison with parents.

Student Name: Betsy McClure	Grade:10
Specific Learning Disability	Case Coordinator: Susan Fitzell

Strengths

Avg. Intelligence, Verbal Reasoning Skills, Athletic Ability, Social Skills

Area where student will experience most difficulty
- Remembering spoken instructions
- Slow reading speed (reading at 4.8 grade level)
- Comprehending text/questions
- Reluctant to read aloud
- Research/study skills
- Spelling, Handwriting
- Taking dictation, copying, particularly from board or overhead projector
- Organizing/structuring written work
- Lack of confidence and self esteem

Classroom adaptations
- Write down assignments, instructions (check readability level).
- Ask student to repeat instructions to you, to buddy.
- Allow extra time to complete reading, tests, class assignments.
- Involve in one on one or small group instruction.
- Use Books on Tape and Lectures on Tape.
- Read aloud to the class/student.
- Provide copy of notes, use buddy paper.
- Encourage use of Word Processing Software with Auditory Feedback.
- Use Organizers for research and study skills.
- Use Spelling tools: color, index cards, proof reader buddy, spell checker.
- Use and teach use of graphic organizers.
- Use/provide spacing guides: i.e., graph paper, vertical lines, darkened horizontal lines...).
- Provide positive feedback: i.e., Awards, notice achievement, effort.

Student Name: Juan Diez	Grade:11
Specific Learning Disability	Case Coordinator: Susan Fitzell

Strengths

Avg. Intelligence, problem solving, athletic, social skills, persistent

Area where student will experience most difficulty
- Organization of equipment and work
- Demonstrating real ability –poor tester
- Reading, especially at speed
- Remembering and following instructions
- Writing legibly, drawing proportioned diagrams, etc.
- Skips steps in math and science labs
- Self image as poor learner
- Feels anxious, frustrated

Classroom adaptations
- Write down assignments, instructions (check readability level).
- Use a calendar to record assignments or an assignment notebook and buddy review.
- Use color-coded 'notes' (use highlighters, highlight tape, post-its).
- Teach organizational strategies: notebook system, classroom organizational systems.
- Teach test-taking strategies.
- Allow extra time for reading, tests, class assignments.
- Adapt worksheets, tests and quizzes using tools for following instructions: Check box strategy.
- Allow printing, word processing.
- Provide templates for diagrams.
- Allow 'safe' environment for testing.
- Use Organizers for research and study skills.
- Use and teach use of graphic organizers.
- Provide positive feedback: i.e., Awards, notice achievement, effort.
- Designate a special place in classroom to turn in schoolwork/homework.

Student Name: Marty Fuller	**Grade:** 8
Visual Processing	**Case Coordinator:** Susan Fitzell

Strengths
Strong math skills, spatial reasoning, creative, hard working

Area where student will experience most difficulty
- Reading average classroom print
- Reading hand-written passages
- Seeing/focusing on the board, overhead projector, or television
- Taking dictation
- Handwriting
- Copying, particularly from the board
- Drawing/Interpreting maps, etc.
- Listening to lecture while copying notes

Classroom adaptations
- Enlarge print.
- Print or type overhead transparencies.
- Seat strategically – create a semi circle or a U.
- Color in maps, create texture maps.
- Use Books on Tape.
- Provide a guided outline for note taking.
- Use NCR paper to provide students with a copy of class notes.
- Provide lectures on tape or allow the student to audiotape lectures.
- Encourage use of word processing software with auditory feedback.
- Use one on one or small group instruction whenever possible.
- Read aloud to the class/student.
- Encourage use of Cliff Notes.
- Use and teach use of graphic organizers.
- Use/provide spacing guides: i.e., graph paper, vertical lines, darkened horizontal lines...).

Levels of Services "Best-Practice" Guidelines

Accommodations
- **Mild supports and services** a student receives in order to be successful in the general/content area classroom.
- These might include
    - Supplemental materials
    - Support people e.g. tutors, after school sessions, parental help
    - Special equipment
    - Location supportive of learning style

Adaptations
- **Instructional tools/approaches** that facilitate a student's ability to learn or demonstrate learning.
- These might include:
    - Using a calculator during math for basic facts
    - Using tape recorders, word processing
    - Adapted text books, materials (e.g. large print, Braille, Audio format)
    - Modified assessment procedures/materials
    - Specially prepared notes, materials
    - Consultation with teachers, family, agencies, others

In most cases, adaptations do not require changing a student's grading scale.

Modifications
- **Significant changes (> 33%) made to the curriculum _content_** so that a student may be successful in the general classroom.
- These might include:
    - Significantly reducing objectives being taught. e.g. learning only 5 of 15 vocabulary words.
    - Significantly reducing the curriculum content, process, and product.
    - Alternative textbooks, materials, assessments (content not approach).
    - Extensive creation of special materials.
    - Assistance for the majority of learning activities

May require changing a student's grading scale.

*The Levels of Services "Best Practice" guidelines are simply that: Guidelines. They are based on current litigation, civil rights considerations, and the professional experience of experts in the field. District, State and Federal Guidelines must be considered in the application of these guidelines in your classroom or school.

Appendix – Resource lists

Reference Books and Resource Articles

BEHAVIOR MANAGEMENT
Fitzell, Susan

- Free The Children: Conflict Education for Strong Peaceful Minds, New Society Publishers, 1997 available through Cogent Catalyst Publications, info@cogentcatalyst.com

Glasser, William, MD

- Control Theory, New York: Harper & Row, Inc., 1984

BRAIN BASED LEARNING
Caine, Geoffrey, & Caine, Renate Nummela & Crowell, Sam.

- Mindshifts: A brain-based process for restructuring schools and renewing education. Tucson, AZ: Zephyr Press. 1994
- Making connections: Teaching and the human brain., Alexandria, VA: Association for Supervision and Curriculum Development. 1991

Jensen, Eric

- Teaching with the Brain in Mind, ASCD, 1998
- The Great Memory Book, The Brain Store, 1999

Greenleaf, Dr. Robert K

- Multiple books with practical strategies for applying brain based learning in the classroom.
- (207) 793-8675 or greenleaflearning@cox.net

Sylwester, Robert

- A Celebration of Neurons: An Educators Guide to the Human Brain, ASCD, 1995

COOPERATIVE LEARNING
Putnam, JoAnne W

- Cooperative Learning and Strategies for Inclusion: Celebrating Diversity in the Classroom, Paul H. Brookes, 1993 ISBN 1-55766-134-0

LEARNING DISABILITIES
Rief, Sandra and Heimburge, Julie

- How To Reach & Teach All Students In The Inclusive Classroom. The Center for Applied Research, 1996

Sedita, Joan

- Landmark Study Skills Guide Landmark Foundation, Call (508) 927-4440 Ext. 2116, www.landmark.pvt.k12.ma.us/landmark

Schumm, Jeanne Shay and Yddencich, Marguerite	• School Power , Free Spirit Press, 1992 (This book is a gold mine for providing photo-copyable forms for students to organize writing and reports.)
Tomlinson Carol Ann	• The Differentiated Classroom ISBN: 0-87120-342-1
Winebrenner, Susan	• Teaching Kids with Learning Difficulties in the Regular Classroom: Strategies and Techniques Every Teacher Can Use To Challenge & Motivate Struggling Students, Free Spirit Publishing, 1996
Friend, Marilyn and Bursuck, William D.	• Including Students with Special Needs: A Practical Guide for Classroom Teachers, 3/e, Publisher: Allyn & Bacon, Copyright: 2002Format: Paper, 544 pp ISBN: 0-205-33192-0

MULTIPLE INTELLIGENCES

Armstrong, Thomas	• Multiple Intelligences In The Classroom, Association for Supervision & Curriculum Development; ISBN: 0871203766; 2nd edition (May 15, 2000)
Gardner, Howard.	• Frames of mind: The Theory of Multiple Intelligences. (Paperback ed.). Basic Books, 1985 • The Unschooled Mind: How Children Think and How Schools Should Teach. Basic Books, 1991
Gibbs, Jeanne	• Tribes: A New Way of Learning and Being Together, Center Source, 1987
Lazear, David	• Seven Ways of Teaching, Skylight Publishing, Inc., 1991

PEER TUTORING

Ashley, W., J. Jones, G. Zahniser, and L. Inks.	▪ Peer Tutoring: A Guide To Program Design. Research and Development Series No. 260. Columbus: Ohio State University Center for Research in Vocational Education, 1986. ED 268 372.

PERSONALITY TYPES

Lawrence, Gordon	• People Types & Tiger Stripes, CAPT, Inc. 1996
Silver, Strong and Perini	• So Each May Learn: Integrating Learning Styles and Multiple Intelligences, ASCD. 2000

TEST BIAS & GRADING

Berk, R.A. (Ed.).	• "Handbook of methods for detecting test bias." Baltimore, MD: The Johns Hopkins Univ.Press.1982
Munk, Dennis & Bursuck, William	▪ Report Card Grading Adaptations for Students with Disabilities: Types and Acceptability, Intervention in School & Clinic, 1 May 1998

Munk, Bursuck, & Olson	• The Fairness of Report Card Grading Adaptations: What Do Students With and Without Learning Disabilities Think?, Remedial & Special Education, 1 Mar 1999.
Produced by the ASPIIRE and ILIAD IDEA Partnerships in cooperation with the U.S. Department of Education. *VISUAL ORGANIZERS*	• <u>Making Assessment Accommodations: A Toolkit for Educators,</u> Video captioned in English and Spanish. 2000, 146 pages. 14 minutes. ISBN 0-86586-3644, Council For Exceptional Children, #P5376 $99.00/CEC Members $69.00
Buzan, Tony	• <u>The Mind Map[1] Book.</u> ISBN 0 563 86373 8, 1993.
Haber, Ralph N	• "How We Remember What We See". Scientific America, 105, May 1970.
Margulies, Nancy	• Mapping Inner Space: Learning and Teaching Mind Mapping

Product Suppliers

Teach Timer-- Stokes Publishing, 1292 Reamwood Avenue, Sunnyvale, California 94089, (408) 541-9145

Mozart for Modulation & Baroque for Modulation--Available through: PDP Products, P.O. Box 2009, Stillwater, MN 55082 (651) 439-8865. www.pdppro.com/

Circle of Friends--Content: Part I Judith's Story, Part II The Circle Procedure, Marsha Forest and Jack Pearpoint present information about building circles of friends. Length: Part I - 24 minutes, Part II - 30 minutes. Order From: Center for Ministry with Disabled People Service and Training Resources, Dayton, OH 45469. (513) 227-4325 Cost: $30.00

---

[1] "Mind Map" is a registered trademark of the Buzan Organization 1990.

Catalogues for Recorded Book Loans, Rentals and Sales

Audio books combine important ingredients in creating a successful lifelong reader.
Audio books:

- Motivate students to read.
- Allow students to enjoy a book at their interest level that might be above their reading level.
- Allow slower readers to participate in class activities
- Provide a way to learn the patterns of language, learn expressions, and increase vocabulary.
- Are good examples of fluent reading for children, young adults and for people learning English as a second language.
- Build the neural connections necessary for auditory processing skills. Auditory processing skills are required for literacy.
- Improve listening skills.
- For pre-reading, it familiarizes students with the story so that students can concentrate on the words when they read the text.
- Bring a book to life thereby inspiring, entertaining and linking language and listening to the reading experience.
- Build a reading scaffold--broadening vocabularies, stretching attention spans, flexing thinking skills.

Recorded Book Rentals (800) 638-1304 Telephone

Books on Tape (800) 626-3333 Telephone

Chivers Audio Books (800) 621-0182 Telephone

Blackstone Audiobooks (800) 729-2665 Telephone

The Teaching Company (800) 832-2412 Telephone
Sells taped lectures on history, literature, etc. Ask to hear their free sample lecture on "How to Understand and Listen to Great Music", one of a series of 16 lectures on music.

Recording for the Blind & Dyslexic (800) 221-4792 Telephone
They have 75,000 unabridged books on tape. They also sell portable four track cassette players ($99 – $199). Students can get textbooks custom-recorded; ask for information. Fees are $50.00 to apply and $25.00 per year thereafter—all the books you can read; no postage required. Application form includes a form for your doctor to sign.

Roads to Learning: The Public Libraries' Learning Disabilities Initiative
http://www.ala.org/Content/NavigationMenu/Our_Association/Offices/Literacy_and_Outreach_
Services/Outreach_Resources/Roads_to_Learning/About_Roads_to_Learning.htm

World Wide Web Resources

The links below are also available online at http://www.aimhieducational.com/inclusion_urls.html

Website URL	Topic	Category
http://www.aimhieducational.com/inclusion.html	29 Positive Aspects of ADD/ADHD	ADD
http://www.audioenhancement.com/ae/SiteDefault.aspx	Audio Enhancement	Auditory
http://www.sensorycomfort.com/	**Resources for ADD, Autism**	**Autism**
http://www.explosivechild.com	**The Explosive Child**	Behavior
http://www.ldonline.org/ld_indepth/teaching_techniques/strategy_cards.html	Using Strategy Cards to Enhance Cooperative Learning for Students with Learning Disabilities	Behavior
http://www.wglasser.com/	William Glasser Institute	Behavior
http://www.aimhieducational.com/books/spedbooks.html	Brain Gym Resources	Brain
http://www.aimhieducational.com/inclusion.html	Brain Research Sheds New Light on Student Learning, Teaching Strategies, and Disabilities	Brain
http://www.brainconnection.com	Brain Based Learning site	Brain
http://www.brains.org/hottopics.htm	Hot Topics in Current Research	Brain
http://www.cainelearning.com/pwheel/	The Brain/Mind Learning Principals	Brain
http://collabfab.com	Free tool to foster collaboration.	Collab
http://powerof2.org	Collaboration	Collab
http://www.ku-crl.org/archives/misc/hudson.html	Co-Teaching Resource	Collab
http://www.marilynfriend.com	Co-teaching, collaboration and grading	Collab
http://www.powerof2.org/	Resource site for collaborative teaching	Collab
http://www.eyeoneducation.com/newsletters/639-x.htm	Differentiated Instruction: A Guide for Middle and High School Teachers	DI
http://pss.uvm.edu/pss162/learning_styles.html	Learning styles Inventory- MI	Diversity
http://www.aimhieducational.com/inclusion.html	Imagine Teaching Robin Williams- Twice-Exceptional Children in Your School	Diversity
http://www.aimhieducational.com/inclusion.html	10 Resource Articles: Bilingual, ESL, Multicultural	Diversity
http://www.ginnyhoover.com/learning.htm	Learning Style Resource	Diversity
http://www.hots.org/	Poverty and Learning	Diversity
http://www.myersbriggs.org	Understanding MBTI	Diversity
http://www.nldline.com/	Non-Verbal Learning Disorder	Diversity
http://www.pbs.org/wgbh/misunderstoodminds/	Misunderstood Minds	Diversity
http://www.weaverclinic.com/	Learning Style and attention issues	Diversity
http://www.hes-inc.com/hes.cgi/02120.html	The Teacher's Resource Guide (A strategy goldmine)	Ed Gen
http://www.teachersplanet.com/special.shtml	Teacher Resource	Ed Gen

Website URL	Topic	Category
http://www.teachervision.com	General Resource	Ed Gen
http://www.teachnology.com/	The Web Portal for Educators	Ed Gen
http://www.csun.edu/~vcecn006/	Writing Resource	English
http://bulbco.com	**Florescent Light Tube Colors**	**Equip**
http://www.alphasmart.com/	AlphaSmart Text Editor	Equip
http://www.dryerase.com/	High Quality Dry Erase Boards	Equip
http://www.fullspectrumsolutions.com/index.html	Source for Full Spectrum Lighting	Equip
http://www.keyboardinstructor.com	Text Editor & Applications	Equip
http://www.customallhear.com/	Classroom Amplification System	Equip
http://www.stokespublishing.com	Teach Timer	Equip
http://www.hardin.k12.ky.us/res_techn/sbjarea/math/JeopardyDirections.htm	**Jeopardy Game Directions**	**Game**
http://www.cec.sped.org/bk/catalog2/assessment.html	**Assessment Tool Kit**	Grading
http://www.fairtest.org/index.htm	National Center for Fair & Open Testing	Grading
http://www.newpaltz.edu/migrant/grading.html	Grading in Inclusive Settings	Grading
http://www.teachtci.com/default.asp	**History Alive**	**History**
http://currmap.ncrel.org/default.htm	Curriculum Mapping	How-to
http://www.humboldt.edu/~lfr1/kindling.html	Lesson Plan: Kindling - Making it Meaningful	How-to
http://www.aimhieducational.com/books/spedbooks.html	Books on Topics covered in seminar	Inclusion
http://www.aimhieducational.com/books/spedbooks.html	Paraprofessional's Guide to the Inclusive Classroom	Inclusion
http://www.inclusion.com/	Inclusion Resource	Inclusion
http://www.quasar.ualberta.ca/ddc/incl/intro.htm#top	Inclusion: School as a Caring Community (Excellent Resource)	Inclusion
http://www.ualberta.ca/~jpdasddc/INDEX.html	Inclusion Resource	Inclusion
http://www.wrightslaw.com/	**Special Ed Law Advocates**	**Law**
http://tmwmedia.com/algebra_tutor.html	Algebra Tutor Video	Math
http://www.aimhieducational.com/books/spedbooks.html	Visual Math: See How Math Makes Sense	Math
http://www.aimhieducational.com/inclusion.html	Graphic Organizers	Math
http://www.dotolearn.com	Math grids and much more	Math
http://www.fasenet.org/store/kay_toliver/eddiefiles.html	Math Videos	Math
http://www.marcycookmath.com	Zip Around Cards, I have/Who has?	Math
http://www.mathgen.com/remedial.htm	Math Resource	Math
http://www.mathlearningcenter.org/	Visual resources for teaching math	Math
http://www.rogertaylor.com/	**Click on Resource Library for songs**	**Math**
http://www.teachingideas.co.uk/maths/contents.htm	Math Ideas	Math
http://www.tsbvi.edu/math/index.htm	Teaching Math to visually impaired students	Math
http://www.flashcardexchange.com	Create Flash Cards	Memory
http://www.aimhieducational.com/inclusion.html	Reading, Writing, Rapping	Music
http://www.jazzdigger.com/b/Ron_Brown/	Music to Teach by	Music

Website URL	Topic	Category
http://www.musicintheclassroom.com/	Music to Teach by	Music
http://www.neilslade.com	Music to Teach by	Music
http://www.rocknlearn.com/	Learning to Music	Music
http://www.shakeandlearn.com	**Grammar, math, science and language to music**	**Music**
http://www.scienceexplosion.com	**Sing the Science Standards**	**Music**
http://www.songsforteaching.com/index.html	Music to Teach by	Music
http://www.flocabulary.com/	Vocabulary put to Song	Music
http://www.haverford.edu/physics-astro/songs/	Physics Songs	Music
http://faculty.washington.edu/crowther/Misc/Songs/links.shtml	Science Song Links	Music
http://www.applest.com/intelligear.asp	Organizers & Learning Style	Org
http://www.homeworknow.com	Online homework resource	Org
http://www.landmarkschool.org/	Binder & Study Skills	Org
http://www.nwrel.org/scpd/catalog/modellist.asp	List of Model Programs	Program
http://src.scholastic.com/ecatalog/readingcounts/lexiles/index.htm	Lexile Framework for Reading	Reading
http://www.scientificlearning.com/	Fast ForWord;Develops language & listening skills for reading.	Reading
http://www.sundancepub.com/c/@5RKYpnKw1bYvA/Pages/index.html	Reading Resource	Reading
http://school.discovery.com/schrockguide/assess.html	Rubrics	Rubrics
http://www.rubrics4teachers.com/	Rubrics	Rubrics
http://school.discovery.com	Science Resource	Science
http://www.ericfacility.net/ericdigests/ed433185.html	Science Classrooms for Students with Special Needs	Science
http://www.webelements.com/	Interactive Periodic Table	Science
http://www.readplease.com	**Text To Speech Software**	**Software**
http://www.naturalreaders.com/	**Text To Speech Software**	**Software**
http://www.cast.org	**Text To Speech Software**	**Software**
http://www.computerautomation.com/	Special Education Automation Software	Software
http://www.mimio.com	**No Smartboard? Try this!!**	**Software**
http://www.slatersoftware.com/	**Picture It & PixWriter**	**Software**
http://www.widgit.com/products/wws2000/	**Writing with Symbols**	**Software**
http://www.nuance.com/education/	**Dragon Speak- Voice to Text**	**Software**
http://www.disabilityresources.org/FAMOUS.html	Famous people with LD	SpEd
http://www.disabilityresources.org/index.html	Resource	SpEd
http://www.ideapractices.org/	**Resource**	SpEd
http://www.iser.com/	LD Professional Directory	SpEd
http://www.ku-crl.org/iei/index.html	Ctr for Res'ch on Learning	SpEd
http://www.ldonline.org/	**LD Online Resource**	SpEd
http://www.lrpdartnell.com/cgi-bin/SoftCart.exe/scstore/01_Special_Ed/cat-IDEA.html?E+scstore	Special Education Products	SpEd
http://muskingum.edu/~cal/database/	Learning Strategies Database	strategy
http://www.aimhieducational.com/inclusion.html	Cut and Paste 101	strategy
http://education.umn.edu/NCEO/AccomStudies.htm	Online Accommodations biblio.	Tools

Website URL	Topic	Category
http://puzzlemaker.school.discovery.com/	Puzzlemaker	Tools
http://us.dk.com/?11CS^home	**Dorling Kindersley**	**Tools**
http://wikkistix.com	Hands on Learning, Figit Toys	Tools
http://www.aimhieducational.com/books/spedbooks.html	**Mandala Coloring Books**	**Tools**
http://www.aimhieducational.com/brainchild.html	**Brainchild: Technology builds English & Math Skills in line with State Standards**	**Tools**
http://www.epraise.com	Recognition Products & ideas	Tools
http://www.mindbinders.com/	Mindbinders Study Cards (Those cute ones on a ring)	Tools
http://www.schoolhousetech.com/	Worksheet Factory	Tools
http://www.sunburstmedia.com/	For Language Learners	Tools
http://www.studygs.net/	Study guides and strategies	Tools
http://www.graphicorganizers.com/	Graphic Organizers	Tools
http://www.teachervision.fen.com/lesson-plans/lesson-6293.html	Graphic Organizers	Tools
http://www.inspiration.com/	**Graphic Organizer Software**	**Tools**
http://www.thinkingmaps.com/	**Graphic Organizer Program**	**Tools**
http://www.trainerswarehouse.com	**Teacher & Presenter Supplies**	**Tools**
http://www.mindtools.com/memory.html	Tools for improving Memory	Tools
http://www.reallygoodstuff.com	**Wonderful Teacher Supplies**	**Tools**
home.att.net/~clnetwork/thinkps.htm	Think Pair Share Options	TPS
http://www.brainpop.com/	**Video Clips on All topics**	**Video**
http://unitedstreaming.com/	**Video Clips on All topics**	**Video**
http://www.teachersdomain.org	Science & Social Studies	Video
http://www.irlen.com/training_teacher.htm	How Teachers can help w/vision problems	Visual
http://www.nora.cc/index.html	Vision Issues Resource	Visual
http://vischeck.com	**What does "colorblind" see?**	**Visual**
http://www.oep.org/	**Behavioral Optometry**	**Visual**
http://www.pavevision.org	Parents Active for Vision Education	Visual
http://www.tsbvi.edu	Blind and Visually Impaired	Visual
http://www.vis-ed.com/	Visual Ed Study Card Sets	Visual
http://www.drawingwriting.com/index.html	Drawing/Writing and the new literacy	Writing
http://www.stepuptowriting.com/default.asp	Multisensory writing strategies	Writing

Bring Susan to Your School for Consultation or In-service

Susan provides <u>customized in-service, on-going training, facilitation and consultation</u> specifically geared to meeting your school or district's needs for <u>grades K through 12</u>.

She can help your district meet NCLB requirements for quality professional development aimed at increasing student achievement and promoting effective collaboration.

For more information call
AIMHI Educational Programs' management office at:
210-473-2863
Alternatively, send an e-mail to <u>sfitzell@aimhieducational.com</u>
Or fill out the web form
<u>http://www.aimhieducational.com/contactus.aspx</u>
Download topic fliers from <u>www.aimhieducational.com</u>

Order Susan's Books!

Cogent Catalyst Publications

Make a Difference for our Children

PO Box 6182, Manchester, NH 03103 Phone 603-625-6087 Fax (603) 218-6291 info@cogentcatalyst.com

[Name]	[Date]
[Company Name]	[Street Address]
[Phone]	[City, ST ZIP Code]
[e-mail]	

Shipping Method	Shipping Terms	Payment Terms: Net 30 or late fee will be applied	
☐Media ☐Priority	10% S & H	***see note below***	

Qty	Description	Unit Price	Discount % Price	Line Total
	Special Needs in the General Classroom: Strategies That Make it Work	$19.00		
	Set of 10		$150.00	
	Transforming Anger to Personal Power: An Anger Management Curriculum Guide for Grades 6 Through 12	$21.95		
	Set of 10		$219.50	
	Please Help Me With My Homework: Strategies for Parents and Caregivers	$15.00		
	Set of 10		$120.00	
	Umm Studying? What's That?: Learning Strategies for the Overwhelmed and Confused College and High School Student	$15.00		
	Set of 10		$120.00	
	Free the Children: Conflict Education for Strong Peaceful Minds	$15.95		
	Set of 10		$125.00	
	MOODZ POSTER – LAMINATED	$4.95		
			Shipping & Handling	
			Total Due	

Shipping and Handling Merchandise Total:	Media	Priority
$30.00	$3.99	$7.00
$31.00-55.00	$5.95	$15.00
$56.00-70.00	$9.95	$15.00
$71.00-100.00	$11.95	$15.00
$101.00-149.00	$13.95	$15.00
$150.00 or more	--------	10%

Visa/MasterCard#:_____Exp._____

☐cash   ☐check   ☐P.O.#

*******Make all Purchase Orders and checks payable to Susan Fitzell *******

Notes:

Notes: